The Story of The Streets

www.transworldbooks.co.uk

The Story of The Streets

MIKE SKINNER (with Ben Thompson)

BANTAM PRESS

LONDON • TORONTO • SYDNEY • AUCKLAND • JOHANNESBURG

TRANSWORLD PUBLISHERS
61–63 Uxbridge Road, London W5 5SA
A Random House Group Company
www.transworldbooks.co.uk

First published in Great Britain
in 2012 by Bantam Press
an imprint of Transworld Publishers

A CIP catalogue record for this book
is available from the British Library.

ISBNs 9780593068076 (cased)
9780593068083 (tpb)

Addresses for Random House Group Ltd companies outside the UK
can be found at: www.randomhouse.co.uk
The Random House Group Ltd Reg. No. 954009

The Random House Group Limited supports the Forest Stewardship Council (FSC©), the
leading international forest-certification organization. Our books carrying the FSC label are
printed on FSC©-certified paper. FSC is the only forest-certification scheme endorsed by
the leading environmental organizations, including Greenpeace. Our paper procurement
policy can be found at www.randomhouse.co.uk/environment.

Typeset in 11.5/16 pt OPTIBerling Agency
by Falcon Oast Graphic Art Ltd.

Printed and bound by Clays Ltd, Bungay, Suffolk

2 4 6 8 10 9 7 5 3 1

The Story of The Streets

Introduction

A song is a moment in time, but the time it takes to write that song might be many moments when opposing emotions are felt. I've talked about this a lot while taking cocaine on tour buses, but it's just as much of a bugbear for me when I'm not under the influence.

If there's one illusion I'd like this book to lay to rest, it's the idea that a particular song or rap or whatever expresses one emotion and therefore the person who made it was necessarily feeling nothing but that emotion throughout its making. I don't know why setting everyone straight on this point has become so important to me over the years. Maybe I'll find out by the end of the last chapter.

> ❝ *I'm here to tell you that it's just a load of numbers in a machine* ❞

People tend to think that because a piece of music inspires them to feel a particular way, that emotion must somehow be inherent in it. Empirically, that is not the case.

All of us would appreciate that it's not possible for a digital file resting on the internet to have a soul, yet in the end that is kind of what it boils down to. I'm here to tell you that it's just a load of numbers in a machine, but some of those numbers work better than others. And I have no doubt that Richard Dawkins would agree with me that it's in the exact nature of those equations that the true mystery lies.

Because so many more people experience music as consumers than as creators, these two very different processes — making music, and listening to it — tend to get transposed, as if they're mirror images of each other. Obviously there's an emotional element that goes into the song on the part of the person or people who write and perform it, and there's an emotion that comes out in terms of the reaction it inspires in the listener. But where the listening experience is basically one thing, what you're putting into a song when you're writing it is a lot more diffuse and all over the shop.

There might be an emotion that gives you the original idea, but you make all sorts of decisions for all kinds of reasons along the way in terms of how to flesh that idea out. Some of those decisions — maybe most, or even all, of them — will end up being mistakes, but those mistakes might end up being the things about the song that people like best. So you shouldn't try not to make them.

A story works the same way as a song in that regard. There can be many reasons why a story got to be the way it was, but once the story's written, that's it.

‘ I don't know much about Mark Rothko, but I know what I like ’

When I consider a subject about which I am not knowledge-able — say, modern art — I realize that my ignorance of certain artists probably means that the incredible authenticity they may have just goes over my head. I don't know much about Mark Rothko, but I know what I like. And I also know where the vast majority of my modest allotment of Rothko knowledge came from: a TV programme called *The Power Of Art*, presented by that cat who helped out with the royal wedding coverage, Simon Schama. It was a really good show. He took one work of art a week, and went into the story of it.

By 'the story', I mean the melting pot of all aspects of humanity surrounding that piece of art – the story of the artist, the story of the individual work, the historical context, the art movement it was a part of . . . The longer my own personal University of Life thesis goes on, the more I realize that what you do or don't think about all of those things totally informs how you receive the art.

I used to think music was just sound, but now I know there is a lot of story in it as well. To take an obvious example, if you've got four eighteen-year-olds playing fairly ordinary rock 'n' roll, finding out whether they happen to be football hooligans from Portsmouth or mountaineering buddies from public school will certainly inform how you receive the noise they make.

> ❛ *I'm going to be as honest as the publisher's lawyers will allow* ❜

This book is going to try and get as close as possible to the full story of what informed the noise of The Streets. Obviously that's something I should be fairly well qualified to know about, and I'm going to be as honest as the publisher's lawyers will allow. I'm also going to attempt to tell the story in a way that reflects the haphazard and indecisive way in which creativity actually evolves, as well as with the kind of deceptively straightforward chronological progressions which make writing books easier.

There's a great deal of self-delusion in songwriting. A lot of people write a song quite quickly and then they feel like it would be sacrilege to alter it. I suppose they like the idea of saying 'It just came to me'. To be fair, it is sometimes possible to come up with something that's going to be around for ages in the time it takes to boil a kettle, but that's not the way it usually works. I couldn't put the process into better words than those of the man who up until the fourth Streets album was the only songwriter I had collaborated with on The Streets. His name was Paul McCartney (by way of a lawsuit over 'Never Went To Church'), and the words were 'take a bad song and make it better'.

When it comes to knowing what a song actually means, though, there's no substitute for a fresh pair of ears. Even though I can tell you how every sound was made and what all the lyrics were intended to refer to, in terms of understanding the meaning or even the value of the song, you'll have the jump on me every time.

Every time I write a song I think, 'This is an absolute tune', but most of the time it's not. At other times I've felt I haven't worked hard enough at something, but then it becomes this huge deal.

The way in which our fuck-ups can be just as valuable to us as the things we get right is definitely one of the major underlying themes of the story of The Streets. Pretty much every aspect of

❝ It would be wrong to think that I'm not egotistically driven to share ❞

the way I initially approached my career was based on a false premise. It's also why you need really good A&R and management you can love to hate.

The thing about hip-hop artists in the nineties that influenced me the most, apart from their music, was the fact that you never saw them. People like Redman or Mobb Deep or Inspectah Deck from the Wu-Tang Clan didn't seem to do interviews, appear on *Top Of The Pops*, or come to England in any capacity whatsoever. This mystique became very deeply engrained in my idea of how people who made music should conduct themselves.

Of course, once The Streets was up and running and I started to go to America, I realized that my rap role models were not quite as reclusive as I'd imagined. In fact, they were everywhere — doing loads of interviews, appearing on any TV show that would have them, and generally being celebrities. And why shouldn't they? It's not like hip-hop projects itself as a repository of restraint and self-denial.

But by this time the die was cast as far as my own attitude to being in the limelight was concerned. I had based my public profile on the example of American artists who never really made it to the UK, in the erroneous conviction that this was how their lives would be in their own country as well. Add that to Daft Punk doing interviews in motorbike helmets and you're getting towards my vibe. It all worked out for the best in the end. As shaky as its foundations were, the resulting edifice of clannish self-sufficiency, wilful non-compliance and mild paranoia was a place I was happy to call home.

It would be wrong to think that I'm not egotistically driven to share — I suppose you're holding the proof of that proposition in your hand right now. My mum sees straight through the complicated side of my approach to my career, because she knows that ultimately I am looking to get attention. When my family look at old home movies of me when I was young, I'm always really in the camera. Even as a kid, there was a great desire in me to communicate with people. But I just like to control the environment in which I do that.

❛ I didn't map out the contours of a five-album odyssey from the very beginning ❜

There are aspects of The Streets' story which might look like I designed them in the interests of narrative closure, but that wasn't the case. I didn't map out the contours of a five-album odyssey from the very beginning. I could see the satisfaction in being able to complete The Streets' allotted time-span and then move on to other things, but it never felt like the realization of a master-plan.

When you do a five-album deal with a record label, what that actually means is you commit to not making a record for anyone else until you've made five for them. But whether you get to do that is entirely dependent on them not dropping you — which they can do at any time — so you can't ever afford to think beyond the next album, because if that's sufficiently shit, there will be no others.

This sense of head down, shuffling on towards the next one, then looking back at the end to see if you can see a pattern emerging, seems to be something trying to get to the end of a five-year deal and making your way through day-to-day existence have in common.

That is one of a number of important lessons I was taught by the Hollywood screenwriting guru Robert McKee, in the course of a university seminar I attended opposite Madame Tussaud's, in the interlude between my third and fourth albums. He's quite an old guy — in his seventies, for sure — and he wears a big black hat which is so round it could almost have corks on it.

It's a three-day course — twelve hours a day, with one hour off in the middle — and the way he conducts it is totalitarian to the extent of being almost unhinged. Anyone who gets caught talking is instantly thrown out; you're not even allowed to ask a question. The rationale for this is that you've paid a lot of money to hear him, and you're not there to listen to anyone else. It makes pretty good sense, when you think about it. There is a lot of stuff to get through, and the rigorous atmosphere of the event certainly gets to the point and stays on it.

Bob's specialist subject is story-telling. He believes that when this is done right, it runs in parallel with our natural psychology. So it's not a thing that we created, it's a thought process – the way we find meaning. 'Life is drama without meaning, whereas story is drama with meaning' – that is one of his favourite sayings, and it's certainly an equation that adds up as far as I'm concerned.

The way Bob sees it, a story is 'a design in five parts', those elements being The Inciting Event, which sets everything in motion (e.g. boy meets girl), Progressive Complications (boy discovers girl's dad works for Russian mafia), Crisis (boy and girl inadvertently uncover mafia dad's evil plot to blackmail UN with stolen plutonium), Climax (girlfriend heroically eats radioactive materials and dies horribly) and Resolution (boy escapes to Tibetan monastery and ultimately regains spiritual equilibrium). Since I'm never going to get a better chance than this to put Bob's teachings to the test, I've decided to use them as the template for telling the story of The Streets.

Conveniently for me, each of the five parts of Bob's story design seems to have its own Streets album. OK, they don't proceed in the sequence specified by Bob, but there's no reason why that should be a problem. After all, as a famous French bloke once said, 'A story should always have a beginning, a middle, and an end, but not necessarily in that order.'

Contents

I

The Inciting Event: *Original Pirate Material*

1

I'm not a very good rapper

I'm not a very good rapper. I never have been. It's not about thinking, it's about knowing. And I do know what a good rapper is —
there is an objective gold standard — so if you think I am one, then
you're wrong.

There's never been any doubt about my production, but when
it comes to my rapping, it's more like 'He just kind of has the right
to do that, cos his beats are quite good'. It's like Erick Sermon
rapping with EPMD: he sounds pretty terrible, really, but his
words still have a kind of weight — you hear them and think 'I
respect you'. Or when the RZA used to step up to the mic and do
a track on a Wu-Tang Clan album — a lot of people didn't regard
him as a very good rapper, but he made the beat, so they let him
have his say.

Oddly — or maybe not so oddly, come to think of it — when I
was growing up, the RZA was always my favourite Wu-Tanger.
Him and Raekwon. Ghostface took the backpacker route, but
he's still pretty solid, even now. I never really liked Method Man so
much, although I do think he's quite attractive — if you look at

him closely, he's kind of *pretty*, and sometimes it's almost as if he's wearing make-up. I do think Raekwon the Chef is an absolute beast, though. He pretty much invented heavy inner rhymes.

Before him — even on the first Wu-Tang album, when Raekwon isn't so much to the fore — you can kind of hear the change happening. *36 Chambers* is not my favourite of their records for that reason. It's still all a bit jump-up, like House of Pain, whereas I'm more into really smoky, head-noddy rap — Prodigy of Mobb Deep, and Redman, those kinds of people. It's on the second Wu-Tang album, *Wu-Tang Forever* — the double, with the black cover — where that style really comes of age. They've gone in there and done it all with those mesmerizing loops, and from that point on, you know the transition's happened.

Going back a bit further in time, you had that kind of knuckle-dragging dance. I think Rakim probably defined the concept of the knuckle-dragging rhyme-smith (that sounds a bit offensive, but I am talking about the dance). Before that, rap was more like party music, then you had the knuckle-dragging rhyme-smith era, from Rakim to *36 Chambers*, and after that it got *really* rhymey. I guess Nas' *Illmatic* was probably a big part of that process too. I've listened to a lot of those records again recently, and they're so lyrical — in both senses: there are a lot of lyrics, and the rhymes are dense with poetic allusion.

I still love *Illmatic*, but 'Triumph' on *Wu-Tang Forever* is one of the anthems of my life. In that respect, it's up there with 'Burnin'' by Daft Punk. If you want to boil everything down to its essentials, then those two songs are pretty much it for me. They couldn't be more different, but they're both total class. One of them's just really funky, and the other ... well, more about Daft Punk later. For the moment, it's enough to say that the highest aspiration my music has ever had is to be an honest response to the way those two records made me feel.

The UK garage scene — which my first album, *Original Pirate Material*, grew out of — was a brief coming together of two

> **6 To me, the exciting thing about garage was that it was essentially a new kind of British rap 9**

different worlds. It was originally called speed-garage when everyone in London first started to get into it, in 1996/7, but gradually the speed dropped off. I think a few people flirted with the name 'The Sunday Scene' as well, because so many of the early clubnights used to be on Sundays — they couldn't get licences on Fridays or Saturdays because they were deemed to be too violent.

To me, the exciting thing about garage was that it was essentially a new kind of British rap. The only problem was that the actual rapping, at least at first, wasn't up to much. This was strange, because to my knowledge pretty much every garage MC thought of themselves as being a rapper. In their own minds, they were all really into Mobb Deep, but the only way they got paid was to chat about going to the bar for a sambuca. It was the same with drum and bass guys like Dynamite MC and MC Conrad (who used to work with LTJ Bukem). I remember someone telling me he'd heard one of these guys — and he shall remain nameless, so as not to defame his character — saying he couldn't actually stand drum and bass, but doing it was the only way he could make a living.

Rap music was not seen as accessible because it was inherently American. It was what everyone really wanted to be doing, but there was no hope of breaking through and getting any attention once you'd admitted that. There was hope with garage, though, because people were having hit singles from really early on. The paradox was that if you were a garage MC, you had all of the career possibilities but none of the status.

Garage MCing was not generally regarded as being very good. If you're a rapper, it's cool — you're a wordsmith, a rhyme-artist, a yarn-spinner. But if you're a garage MC, you're more like a holiday rep — at least that was the way it started, until the momentous Dizzee Rascal came along and actually was a rapper. Before that, your role as an MC was basically to help people enjoy themselves, and the general consensus on garage was that it wasn't very important. Someone like the Artful Dodger might get a bit of respect from a production point of view. But everyone knew that the rhymes were fairly banal.

I had a very clear idea of how to move this situation on. I knew that garage MCs weren't Nas (and when I listen back to some of the early ones now, they're even worse than I remember them — compared to how good a lot of grime MCs were just a couple of years later, they just sound ridiculous), but as escapist and as aspirational as a lot of what they were saying was, there was also something real about it.

Every now and then you'd get a real slice of life. Sparks and Kie was one of the first big garage MC tracks that did that. I remember Kie had two dreadlocks coming out of his head. Then there was a guy called MC Viper who had a tune called 'Addicted'. As a rule, garage lyrics were all just 'get out on the dance floor' and 'dibbee dibbee dibbee' — it was like one big hoe-down — but sometimes you'd get a blinding flash of something that really rang true, and I knew that was ultimately the direction I had to go in.

You could forgive garage all its inexperience and its brashness, because it was real. In contrast, for me, British backpacker hip-hop MCs were pretty much all lying — apart from Jehst, who was fantastic. I also quite liked Skinnyman. But otherwise I'd listen to those people and think, 'You're really stretching this.' There was that whole very sealed-off world of UK hip-hop that could never be bigger than Brighton. It thought of itself as a real thing, but it wasn't really. Then there were all these people who came out of something that was actually happening, which was garage, and whose hip-hop credentials couldn't really be any better, but the one thing we *weren't* was 'UK hip-hop'.

A lot of those dividing lines have been worn away now. But at the time my first records came out, UK hip-hop had no love for what I was doing and I had no love for UK hip-hop. They thought garage was shit because what they wanted to do was carry on trying to be almost as good as the Americans. Whereas for people like me and Dizzee — and I wouldn't usually put myself in a box with him, but in this case it is appropriate — the fact that we'd come up through that scene gave us the confidence to do something that was more our own thing.

The way I've described this process before has sometimes sounded a bit cynical, but really it was just me thinking, 'This is the kind of music I would really like to listen to — someone who is a bit like Nas and has these cool-sounding couplets but isn't pretending their life is anything it's not.' I wanted to hear about all the weed that gets smoked and all the little adventures that you go on. I didn't want to hear someone from Reading pretending to be Biggie or Q-Tip.

‘ Essentially, it was a vowel-shift ’

Obviously, language and accent were a big part of it. I've got a lot of credit over the years for 'giving hip-hop an English voice'. But in truth, that war of independence had been pretty much fought and won by the turn of the century.

In the early days of speed-garage, around 1996/7, a lot of home-grown MCs were still putting on American accents, which was quite ludicrous, and kind of despicable. Two or three years later, they'd pretty much all turned British. I guess once a few people stop doing it, you start to sound pretty stupid if you carry on. Essentially, it was a vowel-shift — like the one that happened in Chaucer's time, when everyone in England started pronouncing their words differently for reasons linguistic historians have struggled to agree on.

It was exciting when everyone suddenly started doing the not-putting-on-an-American-accent thing. Just having the confidence to do that was a big deal. And I think the success of UK garage played a big part in it. But not using imported inflections and slang was only half the battle.

Nowadays a lot of British rappers are quite commercial, but you can still take it for granted that at some level they'll be trying to describe their own lives. Back then, it wasn't like that. What a UK MC was basically expected to do was describe someone else's life. That was just what you did. And in a way, the lives of the people in London making early garage singles weren't much less distant and exotic to me and my friends in Birmingham than the kind of things Nas and the Wu-Tang Clan got up to.

It was no coincidence that the club where garage as we knew it began was called Twice as Nice — there was a definite aspirational element to it. Listening to The Dreem Team on Radio 1 and imagining what the Notting Hill Carnival must be like, it just seemed really amazing. But going out garage-style was really expensive. We tried to do the flash thing on our own home turf a few times, but it didn't quite take.

That's why my experience of garage, which was huge, was in other people's cars and houses, not in clubs. I've said this a million times in interviews, but that doesn't stop it being true: this is where *Original Pirate Material* came from – 'All this stuff about getting the girl and drinking the champagne on the dance-floor, it sounds nice to my ears and I like that bass-line, but sorry mate, I don't know what you're talking about.'

Even though I designed it to be something quite slick in some ways, the basic vision behind The Streets was very simple: people really like garage, but no one's really saying anything worth listening to on the records – it's just a load of words; American rappers are saying stuff that people care about, and everyone listens to them. So my plan was to say stuff that people cared about, but over garage beats. Although I saw myself mainly as a producer, I'd been rapping more and more because I didn't really trust anyone else to tell the kind of stories I wanted to hear.

I was naive enough to think that music which was rooted in their own reality was exactly what everyone I knew in Birmingham would want to hear as well. It sounds insane now, but the first few times I tried to rap about the kind of life we actually led, I remember people almost saying, 'Why do I want to hear about me? What's exciting about what we're doing?'

> ❛ *No one knew it at the time, but '21 Seconds' was the beginning of grime* ❜

The other big turning point I haven't got around to mentioning yet was So Solid Crew. If you had to put The Streets in a time-line, I would come between So Solid and Dizzee. '21 Seconds' was the first proper big British MC hit. Before that you'd had all those jiggy-jiggy things, Sparks and Kie and MC Viper, but then along came So Solid, who were really gangsta.

No one knew it at the time, but '21 Seconds' was the beginning of grime, in both a musical and a practical way. It wasn't long before So Solid had ramped up garage's reputation for attracting violence to the extent that no one could get licences for club-nights, even on Sundays. From that point on, it all just kind of went to shit really, in terms of nightclubs. This was a shame for all those people like my engineer Magic who'd been doing well out of it and enjoying the glamorous lifestyle with the champagne and the sexy girls. But I didn't care, because I didn't listen to garage in nightclubs, I listened to it at home.

All the teenagers who were about to become grime stars hadn't listened to garage in nightclubs either. So that was one thing we had in common, even if they had different reasons for not being there. One, they were too young to get in. And two, even if they had been old enough, they'd never have got past the guys on the door wearing hoodies, caps and trainers.

From So Solid onwards it was all about raves rather than clubs — Sidewinder in Milton Keynes was the big one (needless to say, I never went). And at that point the music basically divided into two again. On the one hand there was sub-low, which eventually became dub-step, which kept more of the light-hearted, hedonistic musical atmosphere of garage about it. On the other there was grime, which was rougher, edgier, more electronic and basically all about the MCs.

There was a lot of confusion about what to call it at first. Wiley made a shrewd branding move by trying to christen the new genre 'Eski-beat', after his own song. That didn't quite catch on, but the actual tune 'Eskimo' was an absolute monster. Dizzee's 'I Luv U' was another one of the tracks which really defined the possibilities of what was going to happen. That song for me was like, *boom!* Exactly what I'd been imagining: someone combining garage beats with being a really good rapper.

With both of these tracks you had a sense of them coming out of a garage underground that already existed. But the new musical landscape was also shaped by a couple of really fantastic dirty distorted bass tracks, made on Playstations by artists who didn't go on to become household names. Musical Mob's 'Pulse X' and 'Believe Me' by DJ Wire (which came along a bit later) — those were the two the old-school garage fans really hated. And by the time they'd been and gone, it didn't matter any more how much Wiley, Kano or Dizzee disliked the word 'grime', that was the name of the kind of music they were making.

Even though *Original Pirate Material* broke through in the year before grime really emerged, and I kind of watched it all happen from the sidelines, I knew what road I was on, and it was very much the MC path. The kinds of lives we were talking about might have been very different, and by the time they started to get noticed I was already part of the furniture. But I knew that what Pay As You Go, More Fire, Roll Deep, Wiley, Dizzee and Kano were doing was just a different version of what I was doing, which was to come out of garage with a kind of UK hip-hop 2.0 that had lost its inferiority complex as far as America was concerned — and they seemed to accept that as well.

I wouldn't say that I influenced them in any way, because I wasn't a talented enough rapper. I didn't have an influence on rap, I had an influence on the Arctic Monkeys. But the success of *Original Pirate Material* definitely had an impact on the music industry in terms of encouraging it to think that grime could pay.

It was just an economics thing, but economics was (and is) an important part of hip-hop. I'd always known that the record I was going to make had to be an album, because that was what I mainly listened to; albums were certainly the main unit of currency as far as the RZA and Method Man were concerned. And in garage terms I guess maybe there's a parallel with the transition from the very early days of hip-hop, which was mostly about twelve-inch singles and party tunes, before Def Jam started selling albums that had their own distinct identity from start to finish.

2

There was something about taking stuff apart and putting it back together . . .

I was really into electronics from a very early age. My dad was an engineer. In the past he had fixed TVs, but by the time I came along, his job was selling X-ray machines to hospitals. I described him as 'a salesman' once, and my mum told me that was unacceptable, because it made him sound like he ran a used-car lot. (To be fair, he did meet my mum while he was trying to sell her an X-ray machine. He didn't get the sale, but he closed the only deal that really mattered as far as my future existence was concerned.)

To me, that distinction is immaterial, because to be a good salesman you have to understand what you're selling, and my dad certainly knew his onions as far as those machines were concerned. There was something about taking stuff apart and putting it back together that really appealed to him, and it really appealed to me as well.

Later, when I was sixteen, I left school to do electrical engineering at college. By that time I couldn't really give a fuck any more, and I'd kind of forgotten everything I'd learnt as a kid, but when I was very young — maybe seven or eight years old — my understanding of how electrical items worked was quite advanced.

My dad had taught me about resistance and capacitance – how the first simply holds back the flow of electricity, but the latter stores energy and then releases it. I also knew that a microphone was essentially the same as a speaker, just wired the opposite way round. A microphone turns vibrations into electricity. It's a diaphragm that vibrates with the air, and you end up with a magnet which will create electricity in a coil of wire by vibrating next to it. A speaker does the same thing in reverse – it turns electricity into vibrations – and if you rewire them properly, you can actually turn one into the other.

Once I found this out, I soon had boxes and boxes of dismantled tape recorders at home full of microphones and speakers in various stages of cannibalization. My dad had a garage where he used to enjoy fixing things, and it was pretty hectic in there, but I was doing my best to catch up with him.

I used to spend a lot of time in Tandy's as well. When I was little, that was literally my favourite shop. Light-bulbs, batteries – all these things were fascinating to me. I always dreamed of one day maybe inventing flight. If I could just figure out a way of rewiring a basic household electrical device – a toaster or an iron, say – that little bit differently to everyone else, then it might actually take off.

❛ Effectively, Dan was my internet . . . I was his Muslim wife ❜

I think the first hip-hop I heard that really made an impression on me was the Beastie Boys' *Licensed To Ill*. I'm not even sure that is a rap album now – it's more like a kind of rhythmic punk – but I certainly thought it was at the time.

I know I was eight years old because I was born in 1978 and that album came out in 1986. It was my brother, Dan, who brought it into the house (he's four years older than me, so he was twelve). And whatever you want to think about the rights and wrongs of Rick Rubin taking what he was doing with Run DMC and putting three white kids on top, it certainly opened the door for a lot of other people to walk through. After the Beasties, it was a short step to Run DMC and then Public Enemy.

I wasn't buying any of this music myself, I was just listening to my brother's records and tapes. Effectively, Dan was my internet. And since I used to spend most of my time following him around a respectful five paces behind, I guess you could say that I was his Muslim wife.

When I was still in junior school, I had a good friend called Chris who was also really into hip-hop. He had an elder brother, the same as me, and because they were half Jamaican, they knew all the stuff that I'd never heard of. The first album by A Tribe Called Quest is quite a big thing to get your head around when you're only ten years old. And De La Soul's *Three Feet High And Rising* I still know pretty much inside out. There is a lot of musical information on that record — basically, it's like having an entire library compressed into one book.

The way I grew up listening to music, I was never the one who knew all about it; I was always around people who knew more than me. It's still that way today. My engineer, Magic, made literally hundreds of UK garage twelve-inches in the era that EU legislation decrees can only be called 'back in the day'. I've been working with him for years now, but he'll still amaze me every now and then with a choice anecdote about MC Viper. The halcyon days of UKG were still a long way off at that point, though. They weren't even a glint in DJ Spoony's eye.

The part of Birmingham my family lived in was about as suburban as you could get. To all intents and purposes, we were just really normal. We had a semi-detached house on the border between West Heath and Kings Norton. Kings Norton was nice, and West Heath — which was next to Longbridge, where the Rover car works used to be — wasn't as nice. That sense of being between worlds was a big part of the atmosphere of my adolescence.

That's probably why I've never really bought into the idea (at least not in this country) of hip-hop being a part of people's heritage. I think a lot of British people lie about it, unless they're from somewhere like Handsworth or Hackney, which are really in the inner city. I know that a lot of the rappers I work with really do feel very powerfully about Jay-Z, as a person — he means a huge amount to them. But I think people from the suburbs just like the sound of the records.

❛ No one is anything, really, in the suburbs ❜

No one is anything, really, in the suburbs. You have phases when you experiment with being something, but your idea of what that thing is changes quite wildly. I think there's a psychological side to it as well. You'll look up to someone, whether it's a family member or someone at school, and then you'll make yourself get into a certain form of music in order to be more like them.

I suppose you could say that if my brother Dan or my mate Chris had really liked heavy metal, then my life would have turned out differently, and in some ways that's probably true. But there are good bits to every kind of music. And if I'd been mates with someone who was really into country and western, I like to think I'd have acquired a taste for it because I wanted to, and then found my own way to the good stuff.

The first album I ever owned for myself was Vanilla Ice's *II The Extreme*, which I got for Christmas when I was eleven. I'm quite proud of the fact that I listened to it once and thought 'That first song is a tune, but the rest of this is rubbish'.

'Ice Ice Baby' was an absolute banger, though, wasn't it? And knowing the history of that song, it had proper rap credentials. There's a great story about Suge Knight dangling Vanilla Ice off a fifteenth-floor balcony to make sure the guy who wrote it got the publishing. I actually stayed in that hotel a few years ago. It's called The Ballage Inn, and it's in Beverly Hills. Everyone seemed to be wearing track-suits, and there was a lot of velour on the roof — it was quite fun. I remember rocking up to my first few years of secondary school with a quiff modelled on Vanilla Ice's (though I never went as far as having the rat's tail in it like he did), so going there felt like a bit of a full circle moment.

The best one of those I ever had was when the Beastie Boys came up to me at the Big Day Out festival in Australia and told me they liked my stuff. I was too shy to say anything much back to them, apart from talking about the knuckle duster with 'ADROCK' written on it on the gatefold sleeve, which at the time I thought was the best thing I'd ever seen. He said that it got stolen just after the photo was taken, in a burglary. It was such a huge part of my life, sitting on the end of the sofa listening to *Licensed To Ill*. The music just felt like it was from a different planet. I guess all rock 'n' roll does really, in an ideal world.

By the way, if you want to talk to a famous musician, remember that they've done billions of interviews and if you ask them obvious things like 'How did you come up with the name for your band?' their eyes will glaze over and they will nod to whoever is with them to interrupt the conversation. Instead, ask very specific personal questions about their art that are so unique that they might draw a genuine spark of a new recollection via the hippocampus part of their brain, rather than the bored recital of parrot verse that they roll out every time they find themselves in Poland promoting a new album.

There's a photo somewhere of me as a little kid with a pair of headphones on, connected to my dad's silver hi-fi system, with the Beastie Boys playing. It's not one of those things where the image defines the memory: the music was having such a huge effect on me that I can actually remember the moment the picture was taken.

Even back then, I suppose I was thinking, 'I want to do something like this.' Although I was already making music of my own, I was only doing it for myself. I never imagined being on a stage performing. I suppose I thought maybe I might have some kind of involvement in the mechanical process of making records, but none of that seemed in any way possible.

‘ The first day that you get a pair of trainers is the best – it's all downhill from there ’

Hip-hop as I experienced it was very much an indoor thing. I was born a bit too late for boom-boxes and break-dance mats. I remember my brother doing The Caterpillar in the living room and me having a go as well, but to be honest I thought all that stuff was a bit stupid. I've never really liked break-dancing, especially as I've got older, and since I've been doing The Streets. I think it represents what everyone else thinks hip-hop is.

The clothes are a different matter though. I don't think I ever thought of myself as cool, but I was barely into double figures before I was all decked out in the shell-suits and the Wayfarers and the baseball cap worn to the side. Pony was big as well — they were the official shoes of the NFL, and the Beastie Boys used to wear them, so I did too. I also remember wearing loads of Adidas after-shave, even before I'd properly started shaving.

One of the things about hip-hop is that there's a lot of other stuff that goes along with listening to the music and liking the sound of it. I don't think I started off with that need for everything to be big, where the whole of your life is basically an opportunity to show out. But I have been around that mentality for pretty much all of my life, and there's a value system that I've definitely taken on, almost by osmosis, as wherever you come from, it's a natural human trait to try to blend in with what's around you.

For instance, I don't mind wearing a lot of jewellery. I understand the sport of it, and I also get the fact that rap itself is a sport — perhaps above all other things. I've definitely internalized that. Plus, I like trainers to be brand new.

For me, the first day that you get a pair of trainers is the best — it's all downhill from there; whereas for a lot of other people, especially in the British music scene, it's the other way round. The hip-hop and indie ethics are kind of equal and opposite in a way, I suppose. Just like amplifiers and microphones: it's basically the same process, it just works in different directions.

⁶ *I've forgotten to mention that my dad had a piano* ⁹

I've forgotten to mention that my dad had a piano. He used to play Beethoven's 'Moonlight Sonata' and a bit of boogie-woogie, just as something to do for his own enjoyment. It was never like an *EastEnders* sing-along. He'd had that piano for ever, and I remember the day he sold it. He got three hundred quid, and I can still see the cash in his hand.

I really liked the piano and I didn't want it to go, but it was taking up too much room. I remember watching my dad play and thinking I'd like to be able to do that. I know he wanted me to get into it, but it just looked much too hard. I didn't have a very long attention span — in fact, it was ridiculously short — and I was not at all interested in putting in the hours it would take to learn the instrument.

My dad was a lot older than my mum, and his musical history started in a completely different time. He was eleven when the Second World War broke out, and he got conscripted in 1945. He worked as an armourer for the RAF, putting the bombs on the wings, and filling up the machine-guns with bullets. But by that time there was nothing much left to shoot.

When my dad was younger he used to play the piano-accordion in pubs, so there was a little bit of musical tradition in the family, but by the time I was born that had completely gone — it was like another life for him. A sense of duality was there in my family from the beginning. I've got two older sisters (who you'd call half-sisters, because they're not my mum's kids), but they never moved to Birmingham when my dad did. They stayed in London with their mum.

Even though I have no memory of trying to play the piano, I can remember really liking the sound of certain notes together — not as chords, just one note being played after another. Now that I can translate it into something more musical, I think the interval I especially liked was a minor third; if you played one note and then the next one three keys away, it just made you feel good. The octave was the same, where you'd play a bass C and then the same note again, only higher up.

As I got a bit older, I'd get given hand-held Casio keyboards for Christmas. They had these little sequencers so you could make your own little patterns — you'd play a sequence of notes once and then it would repeat them endlessly. After I'd come up with something I thought sounded good, I'd press the record button on the cassette machine. At the same time I'd be finding bits of Run DMC songs I especially liked, and making loops of them.

This was from the age of eight onwards, so cutting up other people's songs and coming up with stuff of my own went hand in hand from the very beginning. I think what had drawn me to the way hip-hop sounded was a sense that the way the music was physically put together had more to do with electronics than it did with the piano in the corner of the room. It was accessible to me — I think that's what it was: I could try to come up with my own version of it, just like the people in Chicago who tried to make disco records using cheap synthesizers and ended up with house music.

❛ Pulling that joystick port out bankrupts this family ❜

Hip-hop does not exist in a vacuum. The whole point of it is that it's made out of other music. So even though the first tunes I attempted to write were probably trying really hard to sound like Tone Loc's 'Wild Thing' or LL Cool J's 'Radio', the source material was a lot broader than that. I was lucky enough to have access to my brother's *Now That's What I Call Music!* compilations, and I used to especially love the intro to 'China In Your Hand' by T'Pau (I think that was on *Now . . . 10*). I was a bit ashamed of liking that so much — it felt like a dirty little secret at the time — but I'd record it over and over again, holding the pause button down and then counting on from the end of the previous track (which I think was by The Style Council) before releasing it to try and get the *dun dun dun dun dun dun da dun* without too much of the singing. Then I'd work out how to get the beat from the Casio keyboard roughly in time, and I'd be away.

Obviously other people had already discovered this technique – I'm not going to claim to be the first – but as far as I was concerned, it was quite pioneering. And because I didn't know anyone else had done it before me, it was just as exciting as if I had invented it myself. I recorded a hell of a lot of tapes this way. Obviously you'd get the C30s, C60s and C90s, which were the standard blank audio cassettes, but I used to use a lot of the fifteen-minute tapes you'd get for putting software on Spectrum computers.

Mine was probably the first generation where kids expected to have a computer in the house, but they still had a certain amount of mystique attached to them as items of machinery. I remember being absolutely terrified of ours. It wasn't something I could really get my teeth into. It was just a scary expensive thing which took ages to load, and if you ever pulled the joystick port out while it was on, the whole computer would have to be repaired and it would cost millions. Dad gave us the impression that 'pulling that joystick port out bankrupts this family', but I did it anyway. Only twice, though.

‘ *Let's just say that 'cat' and 'fat' would probably have been the rhyming words* ’

Luckily, by that stage I'd invented multi-track recording, by getting two tape recorders and bouncing back and forth between them. A short while later I got my own four-track recorder. And being able to record myself playing the guitar over the intro to

Snoop Doggy Dogg's 'Murder Was The Case' more than compensated for the pain of eventually discovering that someone else had got in first with that multi-tracking patent.

I did put vocals on the stuff I recorded when I was really young — probably between the ages of eight and eleven. I used to try to rap like Tone Loc and LL Cool J — the giants. I can't recall any of the verses, and even if I could, I'm not sure I'd want to make them public. What I do remember is the time one of my brother's friends from school came round.

It was in my first year at secondary school, so I'd have been eleven or twelve and he'd have been four years older. He was into music — he probably played an instrument of some kind — so when he asked me what I was doing hunched over the pause button in the corner of the living room (I had a small Tascam four-track recorder by that time), I played him something.

The next day I went into school and his sister, who was in my class, was basically reciting my lyrics back to me. And not in the way you'd want the crowd at Glastonbury to do it, either. It was very much in a satirical-eleven-year-old-with-zero-respect capacity. I couldn't really blame her — let's just say that 'cat' and 'fat' would probably have been the rhyming words — but it must've done my head in a bit at the time because I don't remember really doing any rapping from then till my late teens. Luckily, when you get to being a teenager you start knowing other people who rap, so you can mutate from DJ Polo to Marley Marl without anyone really noticing.

3

I always wanted to do music – it was either that or death

I was very clear about what my ambitions were when I was growing up. I always wanted to do music – it was either that or death. I think my mum found this tunnel vision quite hard to cope with. Ideally she'd have probably wanted me to go to university or learn some kind of trade in the traditional way. But that was never going to happen as far as I was concerned.

Because Dad was older and more of a university-of-life kind of guy, he found it easier to be relaxed about it. His way of thinking was 'Get a job, and if you don't like it, get another one: so long as you're intelligent and have something about you, you'll get somewhere you want to be in the end', which is probably true, really. And even if things don't work out, at least having that attitude will have given you a bit of confidence.

I didn't get my first set of turntables till I was sixteen. When my grandmother on my mum's side died and I got a thousand pounds from her will, that was what I decided to spend it on. I'm not sure if it was what she would have wanted, but it was certainly what I wanted.

Before garage came along, it was always a choice between rap or house, and for me the answer was 'both'. By that time I'd already got into making hip-hop. I knew loads of rappers who lived near me, and I used to make beats for them. But when I got the turntables, that was more about house music. All the rappers who used to come round my house and smoke weed in my bedroom called me 'House-boy'.

Because many Americans associated disco with being gay, there was a whole era, stretching from Whitney Houston to maybe a couple of years ago — all the time when rap got really tough — where if you liked hip-hop, you weren't supposed to like house music. The funny thing was, if you look at people in the industry like Puff Daddy (as he was still known at that time) or The Neptunes, they all had a lot of love for house music, but they were never really supposed to admit it.

That prejudice never really existed in this country, because we had the template of the acid house rave, where the two sides kind of came together. And outside London, once you got old enough to go out and party, that basically meant going to house clubs anyway. There was a little bit of drum and bass and the odd break-beat flying around, but pretty much all the music I'd hear if I went out at night would be one variant of house or another.

‘ *On Saturday it was called ‘Fun’ and on Friday it was ‘Slag’* ’

In Birmingham, that probably meant more handbag than hardcore. There was a club called The Steering Wheel which was the place that gave rise to 'Weak Become Heroes' and 'Blinded By The Lights'. In my head, that's where those songs happened. It was near The Arcadian, which is a development in Birmingham city centre, and it's not even a nightclub any more — I think it's been turned into a Chinese restaurant.

The whole central area of Birmingham has been redeveloped now, and it's much nicer than it used to be. When I was young, it was still totally 1960s brutalist. It was just awful really — a load of rowdy pubs, and a lot of street robbery.

By the time I was old enough to go out at night, in the mid-1990s, Broad Street and Brindley Place, which is down by the canal, were the main places where people would go to party, but basically you had to have a job to be able to afford them. Everyone who had left school and found nine-to-five employment went there. But people with no money — by which I mean a tenner for the whole night, tops — used to go to The Steering Wheel.

On Saturday it was called 'Fun' and on Friday it was 'Slag', which was kind of a gay club. Well, it was and it wasn't. Dance music was just getting established in Birmingham at that point, and house was still quite a gay thing, although it isn't so much any more. So half the crowd were pilled-up geezers who were being really nice to each other, and the other half were gay. It was a big mix, very open and Ecstasy-fuelled, so the divide between the two groups wasn't really an issue: it didn't need to be patrolled. But I was still young when I was going there — sixteen, seventeen — so in some ways it was a bit of an eye-opener.

There was another club called Tintin's that I don't think I ever actually went to, and that was really gay. And then there was Subway. You can imagine what that was like. If I had enough money to go on somewhere else after they chucked us out of The Steering Wheel at three in the morning, I'd generally go to this other place that was a bit more geezery. I can't remember what the venue was called, but the nights were 'Crunch' on Friday and 'Wobble' on Saturday.

People who were a bit older and had their own place would carry on well into the next day — they would be at Tintin's till eleven or twelve the next morning — whereas for me the cut-off point was pretty much when it got light. By that time I would definitely be needing to go home, because I didn't have enough money to carry on doing drugs. You generally feel awful by then, seriously tired, and you really need to step up the pills if you're going to push through that barrier.

> ⁶ *The night before Daft Punk, I'd had an epileptic fit* ⁹

I didn't tend to go to concerts much when I was growing up. I preferred to go to nightclubs and see DJs like Roger Sanchez and Armand Van Helden — they were my idols. I remember Roger Sanchez being particularly amazing. I was there with some mates, and it was just a really good party.

Daft Punk, on the other hand, I went to on my own. I told everyone I knew about the gig, but either they couldn't afford it or it wasn't at the top of their list of priorities. But I was determined to go because I was obsessed with them. I played the album *Homework* all the time.

I hate this word because it has become such a hideous dance cliché, but it was just so *minimal*. If you compare what they were doing to a lot of the other music at the time, it's not remotely complex. The norm was tons and tons of loops all piled on top of each other so everything was just rattling around together, but Daft Punk were very concise. It was all right there in front of you. They didn't have loads of effects on everything, it was more 'Here's one noise, and there's another, and now we will play them both together'. It felt like they were able to have a really big, bold sound without actually doing very much, which was a concept that still informs what I do now.

But the actual experience of seeing them was a weird one. It was in the Q Club, which is like a horrible old church where the sound just booms around you and you can't really hear anything. Plus, the night before Daft Punk, I'd had an epileptic fit. That wasn't unusual for me at the time — I had them a lot when I was thirteen and fourteen, before medication got the problem under control, and then they came back for a while in my late teens — but it always left me a bit shaken up.

Nonetheless, I was determined to go. I didn't have a particularly good time, but that gig was still a really big deal for me. There was no way I was ever going to think of it as unsatisfactory afterwards, even though I don't remember anything about the actual performance, and seeing them more recently with the laser show in Hyde Park was probably a lot more fun. It still felt like one of the most important events of my life to see them, simply because of how much I loved the way their album sounded.

I was totally into a lot of other French house acts at this time as well. Not so much Air, but Etienne De Crécy — that video he did for 'Super Discount' where the logo just goes round very slowly was amazing — and Cassius. But I'd never been to France, and I don't think I'd ever wanted to go.

To me, French house was a bit like the whole Bristol trip-hop thing. When you're reading about these very specific local scenes and they're saying, 'It's really cool in Bristol', you don't actually want to go to Bristol, you want to go to London. Because you know that's where the people making the music probably want to go too (though not all of them in Bristol's case ... or French house's come to that). Either way, I was completely fixated on London, and I think rightly, because London is where it all happens.

Growing up in Birmingham gave me a very heightened sense of how casual music is for the majority of people. Not nearly so much digging goes on there as it does in London. Londoners — not all of them, obviously, but a significant proportion — allocate a greater amount of time to finding, looking for, or just talking about the new thing. So if you can come up with a music or design idea that looks or sounds like it's genuinely new, people in London will probably have time for you, whereas in Birmingham they might rather spend their time playing computer games or watching shit films on TV. I can see that this looks like quite an offensive generalization now it's written down, but it was definitely how I felt at the time.

At that point, making house music was probably where my professional future lay — insofar as I had one — but the stuff I did was always a bit weird. I'd be sending it to London labels and they'd say, 'This isn't house music, it's got a sampled orchestra on it.' Nothing I did quite seemed to fall into step.

On the other hand, the hip-hop tracks I was coming up with were probably trying too hard to be generic. I remember making a gangsta rap EP sampling dialogue from *Lock, Stock And Two Smoking Barrels* and sending it to Loud Records in New York. I phoned them up and spoke to the Wu-Tang Clan's A&R man, and he basically said, 'Why would I want to sign an English guy when I've got rappers queuing all up the block?'

That was quite a powerful moment for me. In fact, I think it was probably the point I realized I was going to have to do something a little bit different. It was one thing to rap in my own accent, but another to make music that sounded like it came from the same place I did.

Until the people who are making it start to have a bit of success and become DJs, house music is essentially a solitary business — it's just guys in bedrooms, really. But with rap, there are always a lot of people about, and that's one of the things I liked most about it.

❛ *It wasn't fucking* 8 Mile, *it was just a load of kids driving around in Ford Escorts* ❜

I'd do the beat, and then other people would come in and do the verses. We used to get very stoned, and it was quite exciting as there was always a lot going on. I didn't rap much myself at first, but I developed an understanding of the charisma and commitment that are required to become a rapper.

In Birmingham there are two really strong musical cultures, heavy rock and reggae. If you make either of those two kinds of music and you come from where I came from, there is probably a lengthy pecking order, and ranks to rise up through. But as far as what we were trying to do was concerned, there wasn't too much competition.

We went to loads of the kind of open mic nights where it almost turns into a fight. There were a few other rap groups around, all of whom we knew. One of them was called MSI and they had a record out, so they were quite revered. But it wasn't fucking 8 *Mile*, it was just a load of kids driving around in Ford Escorts smoking extremely strong skunk, turning up at bars and trying to buy a beer but not really being able to afford one.

‘ *Being a teenager in Birmingham in the nineties was really dangerous* ’

The great thing about the social side of hip-hop is that if there are enough of you, you don't feel unsafe. Being a teenager in Birmingham in the nineties was really dangerous. First, there was the pub thing, which could be quite threatening. Despite my confidence onstage – and I am really confident about performing, now – I always found pubs really intimidating. I've talked about being in them a lot in songs, but I suppose that's partly because they always made me so uneasy.

Alongside that, there was all the usual hooligan-type stuff going on. Stone Island, CP Company . . . that was the uniform; basically, it was casuals wearing the kind of expensive designer clothes that only football hooligans wear. I supported Birmingham City, because being a Blue-nose was a big part of the tribal landscape when I was growing up, but I was never really into football.

Above and beyond both those things was the fact that I used to get robbed a lot. Walking around town as a kid, you'd just get people demanding money off you all the time. It wasn't that I particularly looked like I had money, even in my Puma Clydes, but when you're fourteen and you're not the kind of kid who's gonna carry a knife, what else can you do other than hand it over? I was quite slight, and I can still remember the bad feeling I used to have getting on buses. It really affected me psychologically.

That's why I've always found it strange when people talk about British kids who are into hip-hop fantasizing about the American gangsta rap lifestyle. It's not so much a question of people finding the idea that Snoop Dogg might have shot someone really glamorous, it's more that the atmospheres they actually live in make it reassuring to see the dangers of being out in the streets blown up into something that feels more like being in a film. If you see or hear something which captures exactly what it feels like to have a ten-pound note taken off you by a couple of bigger kids on the bus, that's not entertainment, it's just a bit depressing.

There were a few years when life just felt really hairy, and I was scared on many occasions. This might seem strange to anyone who hasn't lived through it, but when you're at that age the dangers are very real, statistically. And in terms of the balance between going out to hear a particular kind of music and listening to it at home, the relative likelihood of getting robbed or beaten up is obviously going to play a part in any common-sense decision about which option to go for.

I wasn't the only one making that calculation. A lot of my friends who came from Caribbean backgrounds weren't really into house, but they would still come out to the house clubs because it was just so easy. There was also The Institute, which hosted the drum and bass night in Birmingham, but that was a lot harder to access.

I love drum and bass, especially the really dark stuff, and listening to Micky Finn tapes definitely informed The Streets, but when you went to The Institute the atmosphere could get quite heavy. It was mainly just skunk, but on the edges and in the corners, people were smoking crack. I wasn't really into that (at least, not at the time). It seemed a much better idea to take the kind of drugs that made everyone love each other. Apart from anything else, it was safer.

By the time garage — at least, the real MC stuff — came along, the idea of experiencing that in a club was pretty much out of the question. Garage was quite on the edge in Birmingham. I remember speaking to Kano about it a few years afterwards and admitting that even though I knew all the tunes, I never really went to garage clubs because, to be honest, I was a bit scared. I asked him if MCing at those raves was as frightening as it looked, and he said Birmingham was always much worse than London.

I thought London MCs would just take all that in their stride, but even they saw it as out of the ordinary. I remember one night at the Q Club where the place just got completely rushed; they had to lock everyone in and the whole event was a bit of a nightmare. That kind of thing just didn't happen when Daft Punk were playing.

4

I don't think they thought the music industry had any kind of commercial future

When I left school to do engineering at Sutton Coldfield College, no one else I knew went there. Because it was the other side of town, it was a completely different vibe — slightly posher, maybe, and just generally alien. The journey was the full length of Birmingham from south to north — it was like going from Brixton to Barnet in London. So that helped keep me at one remove from everyone else. And it was quite a disparate group of people who went there anyway. They didn't really know each other to start with, and didn't end up friends at the end.

Sutton Coldfield College was not a rich source of anecdotes. Finding out afterwards that Cat Deeley went there, but not being sure if she was in a year above or below me — that's about as good as it gets. Luckily, I only had to go in for about sixteen hours a week. At that time I was so obsessed with music that, apart from weekends at The Steering Wheel and working a couple of nights a week at Burger King, I spent pretty much all the rest of my time at home making tunes.

At the end of the two years I only did half my final exam and didn't collect the paperwork for my BTEC national diploma. I knew that a certificate wasn't going to be any use to me. My dream was to start a house label, and the plan was to get a grant of £1,500 start-up money from the Prince's Trust. You had to be on the dole to get one, and I spent six months doing what you have to do — going to meetings every week with unemployed builders and people who want to do gardening. But when the time came for the final assessment, they just turned me down flat. They said it wasn't viable. I don't think they thought the music industry had any kind of commercial future (and in retrospect, they might've had a point).

‘ I got a job with the Highways Agency, putting letters in envelopes ’

After wasting half a year of my life chasing that grant, it occurred to me that if I'd just gone out and got a job instead I could have probably earned a lot more than £1,500 in the same amount of time. That was an awful realization. I'd always been wary of working full-time. I felt that once I did that I'd probably be doing it for ever and I'd never get the chance to make the music happen. But I really needed the money to buy equipment, and by that time the pressure from my mum was incredible, so I got a job with the Highways Agency, putting letters in envelopes.

It was in Five Ways — above Tesco, at the end of Broad St — so at least it was handy for the kind of bars people with jobs went to. It was a really shit job, though, and by the time I'd been doing it for eight or nine months I'd become quite sad about my life and the possibilities, or lack of them, my future held. All this time I'd been making tunes furiously and sending them down to big garage labels like Ice Cream and Public Demand (the chat with the

Wu-Tang Clan's A&R man also took place around this time), but I didn't really seem to be getting anywhere.

Plus, a lot of bad things seemed to be happening. There was a guy we knew who'd gone to jail and when he came out he ended up jumping, or being pushed, off a block of flats. All the rappers I was hanging out with were really into making music but we were just repeating the same old rituals of going out and almost getting into fights, none of us getting anywhere. There was a lot of weed being smoked as well. It was constant – weed, weed, weed – and I could see it starting to take a toll on my friends' mental states. It was making people negative; no one was having any fun. In a strange way, I remember feeling threatened – not by anyone or anything in particular, just by Birmingham as a whole, really.

At this point I made what turned out to be an inspired decision. I went to Australia for a year, where the weather was fantastic and everyone I met seemed to be on holiday.

I'd never even been away with a gang of mates. I never felt I could justify spending the money when there were samplers and drum machines to be saved up for. People I knew at college had gone to Ibiza, and they'd obviously had the time of their lives, but they used to come back with £1,500 of debt on their credit cards. It wasn't like they had full-time jobs either, and it takes a lot of hours at Burger King to pay that kind of bill off.

> **⁶ I thought going travelling in Australia was pretty much the most uncool thing you could possibly do ⁹**

I can testify now to the joys that are to be had in Ibiza – I've definitely made up for the initial shortfall in that area since. But when I went to Australia, it wasn't because I was chasing a fantasy of the Antipodean good life, it was more for want of anything better to do.

I'd met a girl when I was stuffing envelopes for the Highways Agency. Her name was Mary. (You'll notice I have allowed her the luxury of an individual identity, which is more than Bob Dylan would: in his book *Chronicles* all the women in his life just get interchangeably called 'the wife'.) She was the receptionist at the office — they always put the glamorous ones on reception. We weren't really suited to each other, but I guess it was kind of a relationship.

Mary had a lot going on in her life that she wanted to get away from, and she'd decided before we got together that she was going to go travelling in Australia. I was with her for a few months in the build-up to her setting off, but then once she actually went, I became really sad. We weren't even all that close. It was more a function of my loneliness at the time, and probably hers as well, but because we'd seen quite a lot of each other, after she got there she used to phone me.

I thought going travelling in Australia was pretty much the most uncool thing you could possibly do. It just seemed really middle-class and hippyish. But seeing how down I'd got — and I was virtually beside myself — my dad said, 'Why don't you go? Just fly out there for a month, and if you don't like it, come home.' It was probably the best advice I've ever been given. A lot of dads would've probably said, 'Keep your head down and stick with what you're doing.' I'm still grateful now that he took a different view.

After applying for my twelve months' backpacker visa, I took some of the money I'd been saving up for studio equipment and bought an air ticket with it. I'd never been on a long flight before — I'd been to Holland and Belgium, but no further than that — and as I was flying into Cairns, I had an epileptic fit on the plane. When I woke up, I was in first class, which was pretty cool, but I didn't really get to enjoy it because I had a banging headache. A grand mal seizure is not an upgrade strategy I'd recommend. In fact, if you wanted a working definition of the word 'butters', how I felt in that first-class seat would probably cover it.

I came off the plane in a wheelchair, which might've been a bad omen, but in the end didn't turn out to be. Mary met me, and we got the bus to Port Douglas in North Queensland and messed about there for a while, drinking beer. Quite quickly, within about a week of me arriving, it was clear that we had very different ideas of what we wanted to do. She was much more focused on travelling and really wanted to head on to Darwin, whereas my aim was to get pissed every day and go out all the time. There was no kind of animosity about it, we just went our separate ways.

In the early days of The Streets, when I first started to do interviews, some journalists jumped to the conclusion that I'd gone to Australia on some kind of great love-struck mission, and maybe everything that happened subsequently was a consequence of this girl having dumped me. I didn't actively encourage them to think that, but I didn't do much to put them straight either. It wasn't true, though.

First of all because, if I'm very honest — and the reason I haven't admitted this before is because I didn't want to come across as a twat — it was probably me that finished with her. But second, and more importantly, because me going to Australia was more about my life and the feeling that there was nothing going on in it than it was about our relationship. I think it was the same for Mary as well: she was just trying to escape her life in England, and having me around wasn't necessarily going to help her do that.

People love to ascribe meaning to tiny snippets of information.

I do it as much as anyone — not just in life, in songwriting as well. You have to get in and out in three and a half minutes, and that's not enough time to fully encompass how complicated life really is. It's much easier to give people a simple hook to hang an explanation on.

There's not so much of an excuse for that in a book though. So at this point I would like to make it clear that going to Australia was very significant for me in terms of the life I lived while I was there and the impact that had on me psychologically. But as far as it being some doomed romantic quest is concerned, that's complete bollocks.

⁶ It was a bit like going to university ⁹

Port Douglas is really beautiful. It's basically a lot of rich holiday homes on the edge of a rainforest. I got a job on a bouncy castle — taking the tickets, reselling the tickets, and operating a modest un-official employee bonus scheme on the side. There are two of you working together, and if you give a sensible proportion of the tickets back to the other guy so he can sell them again and you can split the money, it's a very effective way of maximizing revenue. Once I'd been doing that for a few weeks, I was just about ready to go home.

My flight back to Britain was booked from Sydney. I got off at the city's Central Station after the three-day bus ride from Cairns and went straight to the YHA. And almost as soon as I checked in there, I met some really amazing people.

There was one guy called Calvin who'd just flown in from Thailand and who quickly turned into a really good friend (he made a cameo appearance in 'Don't Mug Yourself'), his travelling companion Nathan, and another guy called Mike France, who got called Frenchy when the four of us were together, to avoid confusion. We shared a dorm room and we all got on really well from the off.

We just had such a good time. I'd never really been out to the pub with people in a situation like that, where it felt like you were completely free. I suppose it was a bit like going to university, which is something I never did. For me, Sydney was probably my equivalent of 'freshers' week'.

With only a few days left before my flight home I completely ran out of money, so when Calvin said he was going to go out and look for some work, I went with him in the hope of earning a few dollars to tide me over, and ended up staying another eleven months.

The first job we got was upstairs in this department store called David Jones, which was basically the Australian John Lewis, shifting furniture around. We spent the first day trying to move a safe between two offices. I can't describe to you how funny it was but my sides were aching afterwards — and not because of the lifting, which Calvin did most of. There were plenty more temporary posts to come after that. I was having such an incredible time that I didn't really care what work I was doing.

❛ Our position in Australian society was quite like being a Polish tiler in Britain ❜

I'd never experienced anything like it. Everywhere we went I'd meet so many people; the circles were huge. A couple of Danes who were travelling together would join up with three Scottish guys they'd just met and rent a house, and then they'd all get jobs together and the whole thing would spiral outwards until you had this huge flexible web of interconnected individuals. I guess it was like a 3D version of what the internet is meant to be like.

My level of ignorance about Australian culture was quite shocking, really. I hadn't even watched *Neighbours* or *Home And Away* before I left. But it didn't really seem to matter because in the kinds of jobs we were doing you didn't come into contact with many Australians. With the exception of your employer, who would pretty much always be a native, everyone else would either be British or come from Scandinavia or Canada. I suppose our position in Australian society was quite like being a Polish tiler in Britain. We had three of them doing our kitchen recently. One drank coffee, the other drank tea, but the third wouldn't accept anything. When we asked him why, he said he only drank vodka.

A lot of the people I met in Sydney had either just come in from Thailand, like Calvin and Nathan, or were saving up to go either there or to New Zealand. But the idea of going anywhere else never really appealed to me, which was why I basically ended up living in Sydney for a year. I wasn't someone who saw travelling as a goal in itself, because I wasn't trying to discover my higher purpose in life. I already knew what that was — making music. And I felt so guilty about abandoning it (albeit temporarily) that the only way I could justify doing that to myself was by remembering how happy I was.

I didn't completely leave music behind when I went to Australia. I took loads of gear with me. People in the hostels where I was staying thought I was a bit strange because I had all this studio equipment with me — drum machines and samplers and stuff. I had it all quite expertly packed, and I had special padlocks for it. There was an SP808, which is an old zip-disc sampler that's a really cool hybrid between a sampler and a recorder, a Zoom sampling drum machine, and I also took a microphone — an AKGC 1000.

For the first couple of months I was still making tunes, in hostels on my bed — mainly just beats and stuff, rather than recording vocals. But after that I was just having so much relentless fun that the beat-making dropped off a bit. Then, probably about halfway through my time in Australia, I bought a laptop. Before I left Birmingham I'd lent my studio to a friend, who then bought it off me, so I got the proceeds wired over to Sydney and pooled them with money I'd saved from various jobs to buy the laptop, which I ended up making *Original Pirate Material* on.

I was in a computer shop in Chinatown, down near Darling harbour, when this Korean kid came up to me asking if I wanted to buy a laptop. If I'd known then what I know now about buying laptops off people who just come up to you I wouldn't have done it, but thankfully Korean laptop hustlers in Australia actually supply you with real computers, not bricks, as I believe someone on a Massive Attack tour once paid for.

❛ The Millennium Bug had bought my ThinkPad ❜

There were periods during my time Down Under when I was earning quite a lot. I generally had at least two jobs, working in bars in the evening and carrying out Y2K compliance in the daytime. It was the second half of 1999, and the terrifying menace of the Millennium Bug was looming. There were loads of us working for some big company or other, checking through the recruitment software, and they were in a rush, so there was a lot of time and a half to be had. All we basically had to do was go through the programs their agents used and enter every conceivable date into the box to see what would happen.

It would be wrong to say this was challenging or fulfilling work. But when 2000 finally came along and the global computing meltdown mysteriously failed to materialize, there was some satisfaction in knowing that the Millennium Bug had bought my ThinkPad (which was an IBM laptop PC, and quite a good one, as PCs go). A supplementary irony could be discerned in the circumstances of my evening employment. I was working at this bar in Sydney whose (Australian) boss made us suffer for his savage cocaine-induced mood-swings. As distastefully and offensively as I have subsequently carried myself as a coke-snorter, my first experience of the drug's toxic impact on the human character was firmly on the receiving end.

At the same time as this was going on, I went to Central Station records (which was a big Australian dance label, probably the closest thing they had to Ministry) and met up with a guy I'd sent a few of my house tracks to. He was a lovely guy, but basically it was the Wu-Tang Clan A&R man experience all over again, only this time from a southern hemisphere perspective. I remember him asking me, 'But house music is happening in London – not necessarily being made there, but certainly processed and for-matted – so why would you want to come here to make it?' His advice was go to back to the UK and move to London. I knew he was right, and my visa didn't have much longer left to run anyway, so pretty soon I wasn't going to have much choice in the matter. All the signs seemed to be pointing in one direction.

I had a really good New Year, working three bar jobs from seven till seven into the new millennium. I was on the twenty-first-century bandwagon before almost anyone else (except people in Fiji and New Zealand, but I looked to them for inspiration). And I earned the equivalent of £600 in one night, which took me all the way through January till the day of my flight home.

One thing Australia taught me is how cheaply you can live if you're willing to get by on tuna and baked potatoes. And by the end of my twelve months there I'd decided I'd rather just not spend anything and have time to do music, as opposed to work really hard for someone else just to keep myself in big nights out.

By the end of my allotted twelve months Down Under I was leading a much more settled existence in a flat in Darlinghurst (not Darlington, as I often used to have to remind myself, because that's my mum's maiden name), which is next to King's Cross in Sydney, near the big Coca-Cola sign. It's a nicer area than King's Cross, though, like living in Clapham instead of Stockwell. I did 'Stay Positive' in that flat — the vocals weren't recorded, but the music was written and demoed as I was waiting for my time in Australia to come to an end — and the idea of The Streets is fully formed in that song.

The funny thing about 'Stay Positive' is, you can't really hear Australia in it. If anything, being away for a year had given me a deeper understanding of what being British meant. Maybe it's easier to make sense of your own experiences once you've seen them from an outside perspective, or had a different situation to compare them with. Because you could say that the subject matter of the song is the state of mind that made me want to leave the country in the first place.

I've met many people since 'Stay Positive' came out who've told me that it's meant a lot to them at difficult times in their lives. They're generally people who've been either victims of stabbings or, more often, addicted to heroin.

Our house in Birmingham was right near Longbridge, where the Rover car works used to be until it all went pear-shaped. And I guess there was a period after that happened, which coincided with my teenage years, when we all learnt what a skag-head looked like.

People living in worse areas have to come to terms with all sorts of things in their lives, but in some way I think the whole smack thing did inform that song. I'd just seen it a little bit, and I think that move from weed to heroin was a transition that occurred more easily in Birmingham than it did in London. There has to be something in you that is a bit lost to contemplate it, because it's a move only a relatively small number of people make, but I think in places where there's less positivity — either economically, or just in general — it happens more often.

Because my voice sounds really cracked on that song, some people have assumed that this was a journey I was on myself at the time. I do feel the need to set the record straight on that. I just happened to have a cold on the day I did the vocal, and I thought how it sounded suited the song, so I kept it that way. I might have taken the odd day-trip in that particular narcotic direction, but I never forgot I had a return ticket.

5

Now there was an imbalance of achievement

Of all the people I was friends with in Australia, I was the only one who wanted to come home. Everyone else was in deep traumatic mourning over the end of their Antipodean adventure and having to leave behind the easy-going lifestyle that went with it, whereas I was absolutely determined that nothing was going to stop me doing whatever it took to get my music where it needed to be. Before there had been an imbalance of fun in my life, and now there was an imbalance of achievement.

Towards the end of my time in Sydney I was thinking about what to do next and it was clear that the two activities I needed to combine were making music and paying the bills. I think it was probably once I was back at home in Birmingham, getting a lot of washing done, that I came up with the idea of making dance music for money and doing what turned out to be The Streets to say sane.

As it turned out, no one took any notice of the dance music and The Streets got really popular. This is a perfect example of the way the flaws in a creative scheme can be even more important than the things you get right. Because when The Streets started it was purely about pleasing myself, and it was successful from the out-set, this encouraged me to stick with that approach all the way through. Some people would probably say to a fault, but I'm quite proud that the whole enterprise was defined from the beginning by my refusal to compromise.

The most important thing I brought back with me from Australia was an understanding of how easy it was — at least for a young man living on his own; obviously it would be different if you had a family — to survive with very little money. Your rent is the worst thing you have to deal with, and if you can make that, you can actually get by on just a few pounds a day.

I'd tried to move to London a couple of times before, but found myself bottling out on both occasions. These failures of nerve had been the cause of a great deal of personal disillusionment. I guess I was just scared about not being able to get a job and ending up dead in a cardboard box somewhere on the South Bank. But after living on my own in Sydney for a year, I was massively determined not to fail again. And once I got up the courage to actually follow through with it, moving to London was an absolute piece of piss.

Apart from anything else, I had my extended family in Barnet to give me a leg-up.

❝ My extended family is a very close-knit operation ❞

When I first moved to London, I lived at my auntie Sue's house in Barnet for about six months. My extended family is a very close-knit operation. There's basically one set of cousins and my two older sisters and their families — that pretty much sums it up. They were all amazingly supportive, and I couldn't have done what I ended up doing without them.

My sisters would have me round for dinner every week, and the fact that I was living in Sue and her husband Warren's back room meant that I got to spend a lot of time with my cousins Scott, who's a year older than me, Spencer, who's a film-maker now, Miles, and their younger sister Jerry (spelled like the mouse, not Ginger Spice). This family had been my favourite people in the world to hang out with ever since childhood.

It was incredible. We'd go out all the time, and if I wasn't with them, I'd be going up to bars in town to meet people I knew from Australia who'd come back and got normal jobs in the hope of translating some of the Sydney vibe to London. It was never the same, of course, but you couldn't blame us for trying. (The only thing that would match the amount of fun I'd had in Australia was touring, but I didn't know that yet.)

There were also Sue's brothers Graham (who I didn't see so much of) and John, who got called my cousin because he was just young enough to hang out with my older brother Dan when we were kids. He was actually, technically, my first cousin, as was Sue, but she was called my auntie because she's a bit older.

Since this is starting to get complicated, perhaps I'd better straighten it out with a quick family tree.

My dad's name was Ron, and his sister was Dorrie. My dad's daughters — my elder sisters — were Sandra, who everyone calls Sarz or Zaz (people spell it differently; I spell it the first way because that's how my dad spelled it, but she spells it the second way, so that's the version my wife now goes with), and Debs. On Dorrie's side of the family there were her sons John and Graham, and daughter Sue, married to Warren as previously discussed. I hope you're keeping up at the back.

The thing that made moving to London even better was that within a week of arriving I was doing a single deal. I'd sent 'Has It

Come To This?' to Locked On and another garage label called Public Demand. Public Demand never called me back, but a guy called Andy Lewis from Locked On did, and that was the beginning of the process whereby things actually started to happen.

'I can't not make stuff that's a bit . . . outside'

I'd been sending stuff to labels for years, of course, having phone conversations with them and even occasionally going down to London for the day to meet people, but it never really seemed to lead anywhere. I had a lot of phone numbers for different garage and house labels, but my problem was I couldn't quite fit in with exactly what any of them wanted.

I've never been able to make a genre record. It seems it's impossible for me to come up with music that is convincingly part of a scene. I've really tried, but whether it was rap, house or garage, it always seemed like there was something inside me that was too playful to stay within the guidelines. I can't not make stuff that's a bit . . . *outside*.

The song that got me that all-important first record contract, 'Has It Come To This?', was probably my best shot at feeling like I was part of a wider musical movement. But I saw the reaction sheets that came back from all the UK garage DJs: they didn't seem to think it was a UKG record. They definitely weren't going to play it in the clubs – which was fine, because that wasn't what it was made for – but I was lucky to get play-listed by Kiss FM in the end.

Locked On hearing my stuff and liking it was probably the first time it began to feel like my compulsion to do things my own way might not actually be a disadvantage. Garage had got a bit cheesy while I was in Australia. It was all 'Sweet Like Chocolate' and those kind of records, and everyone was still going on about Craig David and the Artful Dodger's 'Re-Rewind'. But, as the imminent success of the So Solid Crew was about to prove, people were ready for something with a bit more of an edge to it.

You had to be quite far-sighted to see that though. I would like to put it down in writing for the record at this point that I'd also sent demos of 'Has It Come To This?' and 'Stay Positive' to Mark Rae of backpacker duo Rae & Christian at Grand Central records in Manchester, and he told me, 'That's not going to work.'

❝ There didn't seem to be any powdered rhino's horn involved ❞

When I first met up with Andy Lewis, I'd just got a temporary job in Swiss Cottage, working above an oriental medicine shop. It was the usual kind of thing — just photocopying and putting stuff into envelopes. I never really knew what that 'stuff' was or where it was going, but there didn't seem to be any powdered rhino's horn involved.

Something they were selling at that oriental medicine shop must have been lucky, though, because an amazingly high proportion of the people I encountered in my initial meetings with Locked On would end up being part of The Streets from beginning to end. A really great guy called Mick Shiner (I've seen his passport and it is his real name) was at that first meeting as well, and he quickly became my publisher. Then there was Nick Worthington, who as well as being co-owner of Locked On was also a partner in Pure Groove, the big dance record shop on Holloway Road in Archway, just down the road from where I currently live (though sadly the shop itself has gone now; appropriately enough, it's turned into a computer shop).

Nick was my A&R man. He'd just come from XL, where he'd signed Basement Jaxx and Badly Drawn Boy, and he was really straight with me from the beginning of The Streets to the very last rites. He's a very mild-mannered individual, and probably less affected by the music industry than anyone else I've ever met who works in it. He and Mick both have this amazing ability to listen through nothing else but their own ears, which has been a real inspiration to me over the years.

I didn't have any management at the start, because I didn't feel like I needed it, and I never felt like anyone was trying to stitch me up. All the heads of agreement stuff I dealt with on my own. I was very determined to know what I was signing and to negotiate my own terms, so that's exactly what I did.

Initially the deal was with Locked On, but then it wasn't, because Nick decided to create 679, which was like an indie label that went through Warner's. After 'Has It Come To This?' came out I asked him to drop me so I could just get on and do the album, because I didn't think Locked On would want to follow me down that road; I thought they'd be more interested in The Wideboyz and other bass-line garage singles. So when he told me he wanted to make my album the first release on his new label, I was both delighted and surprised.

‘ You've got to be careful to get the right tog rating: the thickest possible duvet is best for the acoustics ’

It took me a year to finish *Original Pirate Material*. After six months living in Barnet, I popped back to Birmingham for a bit, then got my own room in Brixton (it was all about the Bs for me at that stage), and inside that shared house in SW9 was where the bulk of the album got done. I already had 'Stay Positive' and 'Has It

Come To This?'; 'Let's Push Things Forward', 'Don't Mug Yourself', 'Turn The Page', 'Too Much Brandy' and 'It's Too Late' were all put together on my ThinkPad in the room I'd rented from this really nice Jamaican guy and his wife, who was a Finnish yoga teacher.

It was quite a bohemian set-up, but not the sort of bohemian I was really familiar with. It wasn't scary though. In my teens, I'd had a mate a few years older than me who was really into hip-hop and used to sell a bit of weed. He went to London once to try and buy quite a big quantity and ended up getting robbed at gun-point. At that stage I remember thinking, 'Fuck! Birmingham is bad enough, what must London be like?' The funny thing is, I felt much safer in London than I ever had done in Birmingham. Some of the stuff that's going on in Brixton is really hardcore, but if you're not part of it, it doesn't really affect you.

This was the first time I'd lived on my own in England. But after Australia I was pretty familiar with the territory of the culinary lone wolf. If it was microwaveable I could cook it; if not, then purveyors of cheap takeaway curry, kebabs and jerk chicken were happily abundant in the Brixton area.

I was so busy recording over those months that I hardly ever ventured out of my room anyway. It was my studio as well as the place I slept. And the link between creativity and bedding did not end there. I was using an emptied-out wardrobe as my vocal booth, and the best way to deaden out all the reflecting sound-waves in that home-made studio situation was to fill the space around me with duvets and maybe a mattress.

The actual recording bit is where it gets really hot, and obviously you can't do that for very long when you're wrapped up in a duvet inside a small wooden cupboard. Also, you've got to be careful to get the right tog rating: the thickest possible duvet is best for the acoustics, but you need to physically survive as well. It's all about finding that balance . . .

Of course when you're climbing back into that wardrobe you are aware that you're some way from the norm as far as studio environments are concerned. Deep down, you do know what the norm is, but you also know that the norm is really expensive. To me, realizing that I probably wasn't going to get it right on the first take, the important thing was to give myself the best chance of doing something good. And that meant making sure first that I had pretty much unlimited time, and second, that I retained control of every element of the process.

I've always wanted to be able to do all of it. That's why I was always going to record myself. My thought-process was 'I need to become the right producer', and once I'd reached that point there seemed to be no option other than for me to do the vocals too. I was far too arrogant to think that finding someone with 'the right kind of voice' could help me. It wasn't even arrogance, really, more like insecurity. I was never going to want to make a track and then let someone mess it up with their vocals. If there are going to be mistakes in any song I've worked on — which, inevitably, there are — I want them to be mine, not anybody else's.

> ⁶ *The people singing the songs about cotton-picking weren't always the ones picking the cotton* ⁹

There were two criticisms of *Original Pirate Material* that seemed quite serious at the time. One was that by effectively making The Streets a solo project and leaving behind the people I'd previously been working with I somehow almost stole their souls. The other was that I was some kind of West Midlands mockney wannabe, pretending to be a Londoner even though I actually came from Birmingham. Like a lot of unfair accusations, both of these charges contained an element of truth that somehow got twisted.

I've never made a secret of the fact that I was incredibly ambitious, and I always knew I was going to move to London. But the rappers I'd been working with in Birmingham didn't really feel the same way. When you're starting out, you're embarrassed to let those kinds of divisions be too visible, and that can lead to understandable feelings of bitterness when the reality of the situation does become apparent. So I didn't really blame the people who turned up in the *Sun* after The Streets became a success, saying I'd ripped them off.

If what you're basically doing is writing songs about your mates, it's inevitable that at some point they're going to think, 'Why am I not getting any money?' Because money is what it all comes down to, really. But you have to sing, or rap, about something. You've got to fill the gaps with words. I was always adamant that I wasn't going to write lyrics about the process of making music — sitting in a room staring at a screen for eleven hours doesn't make for very interesting subject matter. And once you've made that decision, what else are you going to do but look at everyone around you and talk about them?

It's not like I wasn't living the life I was talking about when I wasn't wrapped up in that duvet in the wardrobe. There was a lot of fun to be had at the weekends, and that was very much documented. In fact, there are so many weekends and (relatively at least) so few songs that probably 99 per cent of weekends don't end up being a song. But it's like what they say about the blues: the people singing the songs about cotton-picking weren't always the ones picking the cotton. In fact, the reason they were singing those songs was often so they could get out of having to do that.

I felt a lot of guilt about this at the time, but looking back on it, I understand what my decision-making processes were, and I feel all right about them. I was never anything other than very proud and confident about the fact that those were my songs; I took responsibility for them, and the fact that they existed was entirely down to me. Ultimately, I made big moves that other people weren't willing to make. Upping sticks to London and making an album that was half hip-hop and half garage — no one else wanted to be involved in that. They thought it was weird. They wanted to stay in Birmingham and carry on doing stuff that sounded a bit like the Wu-Tang Clan or Redman.

> *‘ The Streets was about not being from The Streets — that was kind of the point of it ’*

The mockney wannabe thing, on the other hand, never really bothered me. I used to see it in comments on YouTube videos and I wouldn't even wince. When I was growing up, because my dad and his wider family, who I loved, all came from North London, there was always an aspirational element for me in the way they talked. And given that moving to London had always been my goal, it was only natural that the way I spoke would reflect that.

I think everyone who does something creative has got some kind of flaw or insecurity that helps drive them to do what they do. As a general rule, artists value themselves quite low; that's why they want to add value by doing things. Weaknesses often become your biggest strengths. People with no insecurities don't tend to make very good art.

If you look at *Original Pirate Material*, in my head that album was going to be quite a generic thing, the first of an inevitable series of British hip-hop records that would be made using garage beats. But what it actually ended up being was quite characterful and odd. And the reason that happened was because of things I didn't understand about myself at the time but which now seem obvious.

I didn't want to make strange hipster music, I wanted to make a record that would instantly make sense to a certain set of people. But because I wasn't really the type of person I was trying to communicate with — it was the people I'd been working with before (the ones who ended up getting very pissed off with me) who were actually that type of person — the audience I'd intended *Original Pirate Material* to be for didn't really get it.

The Streets was about not being from The Streets — that was kind of the point of it. And that's why the people *Original Pirate Material* spoke to most clearly all seemed to live in Shoreditch and Williamsburg and lots of other places I would never previously have imagined myself hanging out in. I don't think there's anything wrong with that, either. I guess there's another blues parallel here: how many black people do you actually see in the crowd when B. B. King plays at Glastonbury?

I never felt like I was hiding myself in this situation, because actually what came out on that album, more than any of the language or the lifestyle, were a lot of aspects of my individual personality that I couldn't really shy away from any longer. All the stuff that was slightly weird and wrong was what people really got into. And the fact that I was not really aware of those mistakes — or conscious of what I was doing, or expecting the reaction I was going to get — was probably the thing they liked most about it.

II

Climax: *A Grand Don't Come For Free*

6

Essentially, they were hipsters

Although I understand now why my music found the particular audience it did, at the time the fashion element of the situation came as quite a surprise to me. To be honest, I didn't get along with it very well at all.

I realize it makes me seem like a bit of a diva that just as the success I'd spent years hoping for actually started to materialize, I began to worry that the people who were getting into what I was doing weren't the crowd I'd imagined. But I guess that's human nature for you. And besides, when you've put all your energy into a project over an extended period, it's hard not to develop quite a fixed idea of what your ultimate goal is. In fact, you need that fixed idea to focus on when nothing seems to be working out.

The main thing I'd always wanted for my first album was that it would have a genuine place in people's lives, really become a part of their day-to-day existence, and it didn't start out like that. Well, I guess it did, but I didn't really trust the people who seemed to be most affected by it. Essentially, they were hipsters.

Original Pirate Material kind of mushroomed away from

them in the end, but when it first came out, all the people I was meeting in the exciting new places I was going to — Berlin, New York, San Francisco — seemed to be the kind of people who were into the new thing as a kind of reflex. Because, for my first album at least, 'the new thing' is what I was.

I guess I'd naively thought the record might start out with normal people and spiral out from there, but music doesn't really work like that. My music was a bit different, and to people who mainly liked the more American-sounding end of garage it probably was a bit strange. So it was no wonder that hardly anyone I considered 'normal' really seemed to be getting it, or even to know who I was.

To be honest, being suddenly transported into a completely different world to the one I was expecting probably left me feeling a bit insecure. I hadn't bargained on having to hang out in hipster places and meet journalists from *The Face*.

The funny thing is that grime was going through a similar kind of process at the same time. Certainly in London and probably in England as a whole, the essence of grime was that it was rooted in a very realistic place. But once people like Dizzee and Kano got transplanted to Berlin or New York, they became this kind of abstract cool thing for people who read *Vice* magazine to like.

I'm not saying there's necessarily anything wrong with that. I ended up signed to *Vice*'s record label in America myself, and they did an amazing job for me. They're still my favourite Americans, and thanks to their efforts *Original Pirate Material* was actually pretty big in the USA (not in a pop way, but it did spread out a bit from the big cities on the coasts into the college crowd). But being plucked out of my usual circles of family and friends and parachuted straight into the heart of *Vice*-land was certainly a disorienting experience.

The first place in America I really spent any time in was Williamsburg, which is basically the Brooklyn hipster enclave, and it was just a total shock to me. It was about as different to the USA hip-hop had taught me about as it was possible to get. I remember going to this weird fashion party in the basement of the Tribeca Grand Hotel (which is actually in Manhattan, but most of the people there seemed to be from Williamsburg). All these ultra-hipster DJs like Tommy Sunshine were playing music that was mostly electro-clash — basically La Roux and Lady Gaga seven years before they actually happened — and I remember thinking, 'Are these really my people?'

Once I got used to them, though, they were kind of OK. In fact I soon started to wonder if maybe I'd been a bit narrow-minded in terms of my expectations of what Americans would be like. If you're someone who really loves music and likes to get into new stuff, you can't really be like that and not eventually form a bond with other people who feel the same way. It's easy to take the piss out of the moustaches and the mullets and the ironic wife-beater vests (I certainly had a lot of fun doing it), but after a while you realize they're just people who want to express themselves by trying to be different. Even if sometimes that ends up with them all looking the same.

> ❛ *Damon Albarn from Blur came up to me after the gig, put out his hand and said, 'Welcome'* ❜

It wasn't just in America that surprises lay in store for me. Not long after *Original Pirate Material* came out, it became apparent that I was actually going to have to play gigs. This was a bit of a rude awakening, because as far as I was concerned I was a producer more than a performer.

When The Streets first started, I didn't even want to have photos taken. My ideas on such matters were very much influenced by Daft Punk, and what I originally wanted was probably to do something more like what Burial ended up doing a few years later. Maybe it's easier when your music is mainly instrumental or uses other people's voices; in my case I soon realized that maintaining any kind of anonymity was going to be pretty much impossible. The first video put paid to that.

My first proper gigs were at the Reading and Leeds Festivals on the August Bank Holiday weekend of 2002. I'd done a couple of calamitous trial runs in Dublin and Belfast, where I 'nearly died' twice on Take That's old tour-bus (puking in sleep tends to alarm roadies out of all proportion because it has claimed so many of their number), and one semi-secret warm-up show at Hammersmith Working Men's Club. That night, Damon Albarn from Blur came up to me after the gig, put out his hand and said, 'Welcome'. It was one of the funniest things that happened in my whole career. Basically it's all been downhill for me ever since that moment. (I think everyone who's ever got anywhere musically has at least one of these stories. I've been working with Rob Harvey from The Music a lot recently, and his was that while they were mixing their first album, Daniel Bedingfield was working in the next room. He burst in to see them, doing a bit of beat-boxing and bouncing off the walls like he does, then left just as suddenly, saying, 'Well, I guess I'll see you in the charts.')

The Reading Festival show was massive. In many ways it was completely insane to start out at that level, but it wasn't actually that hard to pull off in the end, because all we were really doing was singing the songs. Or 'talking over a load of beats', as commenters on the *Guardian*'s online music pages have been wont to describe it.

There was an element of complexity to my situation, though. I'd never really thought through the idea of The Streets being a persona that wasn't quite me. There has always been an element of shyness in my make-up. Now, all of a sudden, I found myself in this predicament where I had to do my talking (over beats or otherwise) in public.

I guess what you have to project at that point is something akin to the bravado of the school playground; but when you've got to put yourself in the right mental space to proclaim, 'Stand by me, my apprentice' to a tent with ten thousand people in it like that's the most natural thing in the world, the whole thing just becomes a bit more acute. Copious amounts of alcohol certainly help, but that won't do the job on its own.

As luck would have it, there is definitely a gene in me that is a showman, but the way it impacts on my actual behaviour is abnormal — it doesn't quite make sense. I've always been happy to get attention on one level, but aspired to be reclusive on another. I've thought about this a lot, and I think it's a contradiction whose roots probably lie in my school-days.

❛ I did also get into a lot of scrapes involving girls ❜

The junior school I went to was West Heath — West as in north, south and east, and Heath as in Edward — and that was pretty easy. In fact, I actually liked it. There wasn't as much social anxiety as later on, and I was fairly popular and got on with just about everyone. I remember playing the triangle in one Christmas show, and having to say 'Happy Christmas' in a different language in another (I was allocated 'Joyeux Noël', which wasn't exactly the short straw). Both of these early brushes with live performance passed off without traumatic incident.

At secondary school, though, life got a bit trickier. I went to Bournville, as in the dark chocolate. There were two schools on the old Cadbury estate: Dame Elizabeth Cadbury, whose pupils wore a brown uniform, and Bournville, where the uniform was dark blue. You'd expect it to be purple but it wasn't, though there might have been a bit of purple on the trim.

I think I was probably quite annoying by the time I got to Bournville. I don't really know what people thought of me there, but if you asked around I wouldn't expect them to have really liked me. I ended up pissing off quite a few of them and left that school hating virtually everyone and never wanting to see any of them again (one ambition I pretty much achieved).

Looking back on it, I think I just alienated myself a bit. I wasn't bullied — I was never a sap — but I guess a lot of the kids I was closest to were the ones that lived near me who I used to make music with, and none of them went to my school. I did also get into a lot of scrapes involving girls.

I was always able to communicate really well with girls when I was at school, and as a consequence had quite a lot of girlfriends. I don't think girls liked me particularly, but I was certainly keen on them, and I guess I was quite persistent. I think my secret was that I didn't have any of that swagger and sexual aggression that a lot of teenage boys have. I felt like I was the only one at school who knew that girls weren't all gagging for it.

There's something else that boys do when they're starting to come of age. We're quite visual, aren't we? 'She looks nice' is about the highest level of analysis we feel the need to go to. And because we're thinking that way, we tend to think girls are as well. Of course, some of them are. But as much as girls might be into appearances, I always knew that wasn't what it was really about. What it was really about was talking.

I'm not sure how I'd acquired this vital specialist knowledge, because I didn't grow up with girls in the house — my two sisters never lived with us, and they were a lot older than me anyway, so they were more like aunties, really. However it came to me, it certainly stood me in good stead. It also got me into a lot of trouble.

> ‘ *It was like the dramatic turning point in a Shane Meadows film* ’

A few things happened in the last year of school that resulted in me suddenly feeling the weight of the world on my shoulders. That familiar figure of speech had a basis in truth for me, because my uncertainty over what was going to happen next became so intense that it was almost a physical pressure. The fact I was feeling that pressure so intensely was mainly down to a few unpleasant situations where I got on the wrong side of people over girls.

I wasn't like a player or anything. There were just some specific events that involved me really fucking offending people. On reflection, I think the way I dealt with school politics was very insensitive when it came to girls. If there was someone I liked, I would just talk to her and try and get her to like me. What I hadn't properly come to terms with was that when another boy, especially a muscular, angry sixteen-year-old from Birmingham, tells you, 'It's all right, you can have her, I don't give a shit', that is actually code for 'If you get off with her, I'm going to be really upset, and I will then pick a fight with you that I won't ever need to explain the reasons for'.

Certain people just wouldn't talk to me. And the fact that most of them were the kind of kids who are really good at sports and go on to join the army straight after school gave me good reason to be anxious. I never wanted to annoy anyone; there was no show-offy part of me that took perverse satisfaction in it, and I was pragmatic enough to know that provoking this particular social group was a bad idea. I just never realized how upset they'd be by me getting off with their ex-girlfriends. It was a real life lesson.

It was also a horrible vibe. I didn't make them feel very good to start with, then they didn't make me feel very good in return. There was one guy in particular who was a boxer. He went to a different school, but he used to hang out in the same park as me, and I think we'd kind of decided that we didn't like each other. We'd see each other at parties and there was no love lost. Clearly he would have battered me if it had ever come to anything, but luckily it never did.

One day, though, a load of kids I was supposedly friends with basically beat me up. My big mistake was to start seeing one of my ex-girlfriends again, who was popular with some people who were a lot older than me. I turned up at the park one afternoon and ended up getting jumped on by about eight people.

It was certainly the most violent moment of my life. When you're getting kicked in the head, it doesn't actually hurt at the time – you just hear this kind of ringing in your ears – but it can be quite upsetting afterwards, when you have time to look back and think about it. I remember stumbling home with blood all over my face thinking, 'Fuck this, from now on I'm just going to make beats.'

The guy who stopped me getting really badly hurt was the boxer. It was like the dramatic turning point in a Shane Meadows film. There was no real reason for us to be enemies. He just thought he didn't like me, and he probably had good reasons for that, just as I thought I had good reason not to like him. But when it all went off, he obviously thought, 'Even though I don't actually like Mike, what I don't like even more is watching eight people beating him up.'

After that, it was like the cloud over us lifted. We never became friends or anything — I was so inconsequential in his life that he probably doesn't even remember me — but from that point on I knew he was a really good bloke. In fact, a lot of the guys in that group, who all joined the army, were actually all right — I saw them a few years later, and they were lovely. At that point I realized that it wasn't personal, it was just school. Everyone's so screwed up with worry about their own life as a teenager that no one really dislikes any one individual that much, even though it seems like they do. It's all about self-esteem, isn't it? If someone tramples on that when you're at school, there is a tendency to overreact.

Still, it is personal at the time.

❛ At the time it was logical for me to compartmentalize the anxiety with the epilepsy thing ❜

People have sometimes asked me if I think the epilepsy I suffered from at secondary school contributed to my sense of isolation. I certainly thought so at the time.

The fits were quite common when I was younger, especially at the ages of thirteen and fourteen. They basically hit me around puberty, when you're going through big mental and physical changes anyway, and they did give me a bloody good reason to be anxious at the slightest provocation. At the time it was logical for me to compartmentalize the anxiety with the epilepsy thing. The only problem with that explanation is this: I've still got the anxiety, but the epilepsy's long gone.

My metabolism settled down reasonably quickly, and the sodium valproate I was put on stabilized my condition for the next few years. (The fits stopped between the ages of fifteen and seventeen, so I gave up taking the medication. They came back a bit after that, but I only had probably five or six more between the ages of seventeen and twenty-two — including that one on the flight to Australia — and then they stopped again.) The anxiety remained, though, and looking back, I think I was probably able to use the epilepsy as a cover for a lot of unease I would probably have felt anyway.

I don't remember the epilepsy itself as being that much of a drama. We never went to hospital, but because my mum was in on the ground floor with the NHS, working in the X-ray department, the whole process of diagnosis and treatment seemed to go quite smoothly. The major consequence of it was that at school I had carte blanche to avoid anything I didn't fancy. I was certainly able to pick and choose which games lessons I went to — 'I've got epilepsy, I'll just sit over there.'

Everybody at my school knew I had it — I guess quite a few people saw me having fits, too — but for some reason that never made me feel like I was different to the other kids. The epilepsy was never really spoken about, which probably helped. And I think I always felt there were other reasons, most of them to do with girls, why people would either like me or not. But under the circumstances I still think it is no surprise that I should have developed mixed feelings about the idea of making myself too conspicuous.

7

I took their favourable reaction as evidence of my own powerlessness

Once my career finally got properly started, my ambivalent attitude to standing out from the crowd began to manifest itself in the desire to have a respected name. I never wanted to be thought of as one of those people whose highest ambition in life is to be on TV. I'm sensitive enough to be able to see through basic common-or-garden showing off. So my subconscious has subtly tried to disguise it as reclusiveness, which is effectively the most highly evolved form of showing off there is, as you still get the impact but without the sacrifice of personal dignity.

In theory, playing live at a rock festival was pretty much the opposite of what I thought I'd got into music for. But at Reading that first time The Streets live experience turned out to be a resounding success. This thing I thought was going to be terrible ended up being quite a lot of fun.

The idea of supplying the vocal to a track I'd produced myself and the idea of performing that song to a really large audience were obviously very different things. I'd never planned to do both, but it turned out that I could. And not only that, the onstage side of it seemed to work really well. Discovering this had a huge psychological impact on me, but perhaps not in the way you'd expect.

The first time I heard people singing my words back to me was a real defining moment. It hit home during 'Let's Push Things Forward'. My abiding memory is of thinking, 'Wow, I'm singing, "They say that everything sounds the same, then you go buy them". But if I'd sung, "then you go buy shit" or "then you go home" on the original recording, they'd be singing those lines instead.' So this fairly arbitrary process of lyric-writing, which for me had always been, and would continue to be, a matter of selecting words in quite a haphazard way right up to the final cut-off, suddenly had a very concrete end result.

Even now, I still change stuff right up to the last possible minute when I'm recording. I've always had a very strong awareness of all the possibilities that exist to do things differently suddenly disappearing at the point when the final version of a song is manufactured as a CD and sent out to shops. But that sense of 'They're all singing the line I wrote in that moment five seconds before the album was finished' was quite overwhelming to me. The fact that if I had made a last-minute change they'd all be singing that new version just seemed completely mental.

I suppose I was in an unusual situation. Most people in music, whether they start out in bands or as DJs, necessarily acquire plenty of experience of seeing the way the decisions they make impact on a crowd before they get to do their first album. But for me, that whole side of things was completely new.

Some other writers and performers probably experience that initial if-I'd-changed-this-word-that's-what-they'd-be-singing-now revelation as proof of their new-found power and influence. But for me it was just the opposite. Rather than thinking, 'I can do whatever I want now and the crowd will follow me', I took their favourable reaction as evidence of my own powerlessness.

This wasn't a situation that was under my control. They only sang along with those particular words because they wanted to — I didn't know which lyrics they were going to end up learning off by heart when I first came up with them. When you write a song, you don't know if it's going to be the big single or just an album track, or not even get released at all. So the nature of the public's response seems as random as it is powerful.

6 *Freddie couldn't give them any old rubbish, he had to give them 'Bohemian Rhapsody'* 9

I think people have a definite tendency to remove the free will of the audience from these equations. When they see, say, Freddie Mercury controlling a crowd of a hundred thousand at Live Aid, they somehow imbue Freddie with the power of a hundred thousand people. But he only had that power because those people decided to like him. He was just the thing they happened to be into; any power he had was contingent on his ability to carry on giving them what they wanted. If he was truly powerful, he'd have been able to give them any old rubbish and they would still have responded in the same way. But Freddie couldn't give them any old rubbish, he had to give them 'Bohemian Rhapsody'. OK, at certain points in his career Freddie probably could, and no doubt did, get away with giving them any old rubbish. But he could only do that because the crowd had already decided they were going to like it, and they'd made that decision on the basis of the good songs he'd done before.

A lot of artists do a good song, then they do a shit song. They can retain their audience's interest while writing shit songs for a certain amount of time until ultimately people will go, 'Actually, that's shit' and you get this very rapid depreciation in the value they're perceived to have as an artist. The duration of that period of grace depends entirely on the charisma or mythological presence of the individual concerned. People with less star quality might manage one shit song and that will be it. Others who score higher on that scale might be able to spin the shit songs out for years.

Either way, the fundamental truth which underlies this situation is that no one can effect change independently of other people. It's possible to *trigger* change — you can be the catalyst — but that change only comes about as a result of people acting according to their own free will, and no one else has any control over that. You might think governments have infinite power, but they're pretty powerless in reality; all they can do is hope to make decisions people agree with, and then try to make it look like they should get the credit for that.

I feel much more at ease with all this now than I did then. I've learnt that the fact that you write these words and then ten thousand people sing them back at you — or don't, as the case may be — is no different to any other situation where your actions have an impact on the world which you can't directly control (and that's pretty much every situation, because any decision we make, however small — even if it's only whether or not to have another Guinness — will affect the world at some level). It's that thing about a butterfly landing on a leaf in the Indian Ocean and it causing a tidal wave a few years later, but on steroids, because I get to see the consequences play out in front of me in such a pure way.

In the immediate aftermath of the 2002 Reading Festival, however, my reaction to hearing my words sung back at me unfolded along very different lines. I experienced it as a newly intensified sense of responsibility. 'If people are going to be learning my lyrics off by heart, I'd better make sure every word is as close to being the right one as I can possibly get' — that was the way I was now looking at things.

> ❝ *Just go on Amazon and put 'songwriting' in the search category and they'll all come up* ❞

There was definitely a moment between my first and second albums when I thought, 'Shit. I've spent years trying to master the craft of being a producer, but if I'm now going to be writing the songs as well as producing them, I need to know what I'm meant to be doing in that area as well.' This realization has taken me in a lot of different directions, from screenwriting gurus to cognitive behaviour therapy to art history, but the journey has always been about what could help me in terms of making the songs better.

I'd never paid much attention in English lessons at school, but in the months and years after that first Reading Festival I devoured pretty much every book there is to buy on songwriting. I can't tell you much about the people who wrote them, but just go on Amazon and put 'songwriting' in the search category and they'll all come up.

On the one hand, they're just different people's opinions, but on the other, there's so much to learn in terms of male and female rhymes and metre and a load of other technical things. A lot of it is the kind of stuff you can probably develop a skill for subconsciously whether you read the books or not — like the fact that the most important word of any line is the last one, so you basically have to take the most important piece of information you're giving people and put it at the end. But those books gave me some real eureka moments as well.

A woman called Sheila Davis writes a lot of them, and she really knows what she's talking about, to the point that what she's telling you in a book like *Songwriting Secrets* almost verges on psychology. Abstractions, even though they're very common in songs, are very difficult for the brain to process. That's one lesson I learnt from her.

I've become a bit more relaxed about it now, but if you listen to the stuff I wrote at that stage in my career, I'd never mention love or hate or anything like that. I'd deal purely in physical things. So, for instance, with 'Dry Your Eyes' the emotion that is at the heart of the story is never explicitly described. There's not one mention of love; it's only pointed to by physical actions. That's been a key element in my music — always describe the physicality rather than the emotion. Whether it's playing with your hair or playing with an ashtray, when you get this technique right, it really connects — *bang!* People feel these emotions much more strongly than if you'd referred to them directly.

And that's only the beginning. There are all these devices like synecdoche and metonymy which are really useful as well. They're kind of the opposite of each other — the first uses a part for the whole and the second uses the whole for a part. So, 'All hands on deck' or 'I've got a nice set of wheels' is synecdoche, whereas 'From the cradle to the grave' or 'The White House said today' is metonymy. (I must admit I did just have to look up which was which to make sure I've got them the right way round — some of this shit is getting rusty.)

Sheila Davis's *Successful Lyric Writing* is still under the sofa in my studio though. There's probably more useful practical information in there than you'd acquire from a three-year English course at university. And I've got her *The Craft Of Lyric Writing* on my iPad.

There's some good stuff in those books about antonyms — opposites. They're a big deal as well. I'm not entirely sure what it is about them, but the more lyrics I've written, the more I feel like antonyms are at the very centre of all lyrical genius, particularly in terms of British songwriting.

If you think of Arctic Monkeys' *Whatever People Say I Am, That's What I'm Not*, that to me is a classic British album title. Oasis songs are often like that too; there are always a lot of antonyms flying around when Noel Gallagher gets his lyric-writing pencil out. I think it's because what we regard, at least subconsciously, as being the height of sophistication and wit is the ability to entertain conflicting ideas simultaneously. The Americans would probably say that's because we're very good at sidestepping the issue.

> **❝ You can't knock 'By The Time I Get To Phoenix' . . . but I've never really been able to see the point of 'Wichita Lineman' ❞**

The funny thing about those Sheila Davis books is that, theoretically at least, they've got nothing whatsoever to do with hip-hop (or Alex Turner and Noel Gallagher, come to that). They're all books that tell you how to write country and western songs. But a good song is a good song, whatever genre it's in. I know that when he was defending himself against censorship, Ice-T used to say that Johnny Cash's 'I shot a man in Reno, just to watch him die' was essentially a gangsta rap line, and he probably had a point.

I wanted to write good lyrics about contemporary British life, and in my determination to pursue that goal I inadvertently ended up benefiting from a lot of rather distant advice contained in dusty old American books that had been in print for years. Sheila can be a bit of a tyrant about half rhymes, but those of us who were also educated by Biggie Smalls and Nas tend to overlook such uptight strictures: if it doesn't rhyme on the page, we just pronounce it like it does, because what really matters is the overall sound. Beyond that cavil, it didn't matter that the state of mind she was coming from was very much old-school Nashville, or that all the case-studies were weird old country songs. I just used to download them all off Napster.

There were loads of old country songwriters whose work I really got into. Shel Silverstein, who did 'A Boy Named Sue' and a lot of the Dr Hook stuff — he was one of my favourites. Whoever wrote 'She's Got You' for Patsy Cline was excellent as well (though I actually prefer the Loretta Lynn version). I wasn't so sure about Jimmy Webb, even though he's the one whose name probably gets dropped the most often. But you can't knock 'By The Time I Get To Phoenix', and he was only twenty-one when he wrote that. 'Phoenix' is an absolute beast — I've spent literally hours studying that song; if he could've come up with ten others as good as that, I really would be a fan. But I've never really been able to see the point of 'Wichita Lineman'. I just couldn't ever understand what that song was supposed to be about.

> *You'll often hear it said that we don't have any taboos left in this country, but I can name at least two*

I realize that me admitting to having used techniques acquired from country and western songwriting manuals to write 'Dry Your Eyes' and 'Fit But You Know It' will probably upset a few people. But it shouldn't do.

You'll often hear it said that we don't have any taboos left in this country, but I can name at least two. One is our inability to criticize the basic principle behind the NHS. You're actually getting angry with me now for even suggesting it, aren't you? You're not willing to accept that a compulsory insurance scheme and private provision might — and I'm only saying 'might', not 'would' — be a more efficient and ultimately humane way to address the nation's healthcare requirements.

The other taboo is the idea that any aspect of creativity can be taught and learnt rather than divinely decreed. For a lot of people in the British music industry, even mentioning the possibility of finding out about songwriting from a book is like drawing a cartoon of Mohammed in front of a fundamentalist Muslim. My manager Tim Vigon and my engineer Magic are the absolute worst for this, and we've had a lot of really long (and very enjoyable) arguments about it as a result.

I'm not saying that learning about literary devices automatically teaches you how to be a good songwriter, because it obviously doesn't. But you've got to try to master the grammar of the language you're hoping to speak in, and you've got to know what the words actually mean. What else is there in life if you don't keep on learning?

Obviously, not everything in those books is useful. Most of the unhelpful stuff seems to involve drawing very detailed circular diagrams. We're never going to be able to fully encompass the complexity of how our mind processes lyrics by drawing lines on a piece of paper. By definition, the essence of that system is the different emotional reactions elicited by particular words, and it's just not possible to represent that in pictorial or tabular form.

You can't teach yourself the initial spark of creativity — that has to come from inside. And you can't fake the life experience that enables you to fan that spark into a bonfire at which a reasonable number of people will want to warm their hands (like the idea of getting impatient and then taking another pill in 'Blinded By The Lights' — the well-founded suspicion that this was a mistake I'd made myself was probably a big part of that song's appeal).

What you can do, though, is learn a skill with words, the same way a carpenter learns a skill with wood. If you look at the way the songs on *A Grand Don't Come For Free* fit together, it's so schematic it's almost like a technical drawing. I used to really like sketching when I was a kid, before I got into taking speakers apart, and doing that album was like drawing up a plan and then turning it into music.

At that point in my career, I was still dealing with subjects that were easy, both for me to write about, and for other people to connect with. And with the help of my new-found under-standing of what I was doing, the whole thing just became really powerful. I've not done anything that captivating since, so it's not like I've got all the answers. If I did, I'd have carried on hitting that bullseye with all the tedious regularity I could muster.

As much as it pisses my manager off to hear me say it, 'Dry Your Eyes' is 90 per cent technique. At the risk of sounding like a 1970s sex-manual, I'd have to say that it's all about climaxing at the right moment and not a moment before.

A lot of people in the music industry — and this is not some-thing you'll hear often, but it is absolutely true — are crazily idealistic. When it comes to the inspiration versus perspiration issue, all their eggs are in the first of those baskets. I think because they work such long hours themselves, they love the idea of musicians effortlessly plucking moments of genius from the sky. But they haven't read the books I've read — they just refuse to. And it's not just in music that this prejudice applies. A lot of British people hate the idea of learning about screenwriting too. That's why we make such bad films.

I don't think there's anything special about my work ethic in itself. I think it's incredibly normal. What maybe has been a bit unusual is how directly it's fed into my songwriting and production. It has always been essential to me that I should be responsible for every stage of the recording process, right up to the mastering, which no one else does themselves. And I've already mentioned how important it is to me that my music should have a functional use in people's lives.

> 6 *I'm not talking about changing the world here,*
> *more in terms of making a really good table* 9

Early on in my career, I was almost obsessed with the idea that every one of my songs had to have a purpose — in the same way that you build a house, and it has a purpose, or you insure people against hazards, and that has a purpose. I'm not talking about changing the world here, more in terms of making a really good table.

I've never agreed with the idea of politics in music. When people complain about hip-hop or rock music not being political any more, I always think, 'Good'. First, because it never helps the song. And second, because if I'm going to learn something about politics, it's not going to be from some drug-taking guitarist. What the fuck do you know about the state of the world? Just play me a fucking song.

What it all comes down to for me is this: you want to entertain people as effectively as you can, so you strive to make the three minutes they spend listening to your song as worthwhile as it possibly can be. Some people have said to me that they think these ideas of job satisfaction and professional pride reflect an old-school working-class attitude. They're definitely a trade or a craft thing, but I'm not so sure about the working-class element.

At this stage in the game, I don't think any of us can really describe ourselves as working-class. I think we've been clinging on to the idea of working-classness since the Second World War. That was probably the last time people could take pride in the shared sense of purpose that being in a particular economic group gave them. Obviously there are some people in today's world who are much less privileged than others, but in terms of them finding any commonality of interest, it's hard to see how that can be done now.

My desire that the music I make should provide a service is probably as upper-class as it is working-class. Because the desire to be socially useful exists in the more fortunate echelons of humanity as well as the less well-off, in the same way that an exaggerated sense of entitlement can be found at both ends of the social spectrum. I've known grime MCs who think all they have to do is turn up, and they're about as working-class as you can get. Some people will work hard at painting a house, other people won't — that's basically what it comes down to.

Above: Living the dream in my head. I had it all planned out.

Left: Me on the piano. I didn't have the patience but I loved the sound of my dad playing it. I'm getting better, and I'm trying to get my kids into it just like he did.

Above: Me and my dad. I'd never really registered how much blue my dad wore. I think I'm going to try it.

Above: First day at school. I really liked infant and primary school. I do believe that is an E.T. sweatshirt, but I have no memory of it.

Below: I love this photo. My dad looks like Jarvis Cocker and my uncle Brian is being taught about the new thing in medical X-ray technology.

Left: This is how I learnt to drive: from a very early age in fields. The fastest I went in this car was 70, but don't tell my mum.

Middle: Mum and Dad. Love that all-white look with the pulled-up socks. He always brushed his hair, my dad. You can tell it's had a good brushing there. I don't think I've ever brushed my hair in my life. My daughter, Amelia, inherited the curls, though.

Right: You can't fuck with double denim.

Top: Me and my brother, Dan. The rap look gradually started to work for me, but not at this point.

Middle: Me and my cousin Spenny who I'm still really close to. He was always the mad one in the family.

He's just made a film and we went to Cannes. That's another story.

Bottom: Skinners and Levens. My happiest memories.

Above: Me and Dan in the Lake District. Pretty boring place for kids but we came back here when we shot the video for 'Never Went to Church' and a lot of emotional memories came back.

Right: Rich Bitch studios on some down-time. The times were mostly down.

Above: A large chunk of my family in Ibiza. Claire is in the yellow dress at the front, and Mum is in the white trousers. Waving in the white is my niece Chelsea who was knocked down and killed not long after. A stupid moment in the lives of two guys driving like twats that has caused unimaginable devastation.

Right: Me and my brother flanking my dad at the first Reading Festival I did. I always used to pull silly faces in photos, which is embarrassing. My sister has got loads of pictures of us where everyone looks nice and I just ruin it.

Bottom right: This was the very beginning of what became my massive trainer display in the hallway of my Stockwell flat. Up until my deal with Reebok I used to have them all in every colour, but then Nike went a bit cold on me and it wasn't the same after that. I also developed a fondness for loafers.

Right: This was at one of those American service-stations-on-steroids places where they have a full casino and all-you-can-eat buffet. My cousin won a grand that night on the fruit machines.
(© Rod Doyle)

Below: You can't fuck with American customs for seriousness. They are sobering places. This is my cousin Scott who won the grand in the service station. (© Rod Doyle)

My sister made my barbed-wire bracelets and I went
through a few of them. The Local Crew T-shirt is the result
of having no clean clothes but shit loads on sale in the foyer.

8

Effectively, what we did was slap my personality on top of his database

Because I grew up in Birmingham, I had a very clear image of the music industry in London as being run by superhuman creative gurus. In fact, I was pretty much obsessed by this idea. I could see all these millions of people who did normal jobs, and then this other relatively small number of people who did jobs that looked so much more fun, and to me it seemed like it had to be a numbers game. Because they're where they are and we're where we are, that's how good they must be: that proportion of how many of us there are divided by how many of them.

Once I got to London and started doing The Streets, I soon found out that, like so many other aspects of human existence that seem susceptible to mathematical explication, this equation didn't quite hold up. It wasn't that people in the music industry didn't work hard, because they did; it's just that they didn't have quite the same stratospheric levels of commitment as me. You expect people at record labels to have creative solutions to problems, but as a general rule they're quite happy to settle for the one they can get away with.

I'm not blaming them for that — they're only human, and it was probably only my youthful naivety that led me to imbue them with superpowers of aesthetic judgement and artistic daring. Luckily, rather than slumping into an abyss of bitterness and disillusionment, my sense of disappointment motivated me to seek out and then sustain professional relationships with the small number of people I came across who did actually live up to my unrealistic standards. I guess there was an element of luck involved as well, in that I came across a handful of people in the very early stages of The Streets with the staying power to stick the whole thing out from beginning to end.

Even though I was responsible for every element of the music, The Streets was anything but a one-man band. As well as Nick Worthington, Mick Shiner, my manager Tim Vigon and The Beats' co-founder Ted Mayhem — we'll get to those last two later — there was one other key individual who helped establish the tone of the whole enterprise. His name was (and is) Alan Parkes. I'm not sure what his official job title would be, but in my case his main role was to commission music videos and artwork for Warner's.

I seemed to be destined to latch on to people who did good shit, and Alan was both a symptom and a cause of that happy state of affairs. When a new Streets album was coming out, it was his job to make sure the videos and artwork complemented the music in the right way, so the whole package would hang together properly. I worked out from quite early on that he really knew his stuff when it came to design and art and photography and film, and often the choices we made were his original ideas filtered down through my opinions.

Effectively, what we did was slap my personality on top of his database. For example, it was Alan who came up with Ewen Spencer, who took all the photos for the first three albums and inspired the other two as well — although by that point we couldn't afford him any more, because he'd become a superstar fashion photographer. Most of the Streets' videos were down to me and Alan too, apart from the more home-made ones right at the end. It was also Alan who brought in Adam Smith (who's also done all The Chemical Brothers' visuals, including the Flashing Calamari of Hope). Adam made the film of the kids on bikes going over the Millennium Bridge for us, as well as the special video for 'The Irony Of It All' that was originally only supposed to be projected at live shows.

Right from the start I felt incredibly drawn to Alan and his judgement, so I'd like to be able to come up with an amazing capsule description for him, like the one his fellow Scot Bill Drummond had for the radio plugger in the KLF book, who never raised his voice in a meeting but took out his immense anger on his Jaguar whenever it broke down on the M1. Unfortunately, I don't know him well enough.

It's not just me, no one seems to know that much about Alan. He was probably in his late thirties when I first met him. He's got the kind of Scottish accent that sounds Scottish to Londoners but Londony to Scots, and he now lives over the border and commutes down south only when he needs to. He seems to live the life of a creative priest.

Maybe I'm intrigued by people who don't share their private story. It seems committed, which is all I really care about in people I work with. Nick Worthington is like that. He could be enduring the worst kind of divorce unfolding on his BlackBerry and he'd still be at the video meeting without mention of it. He's the kind who went to Shoom back in the day without doing drugs but said the music was amazing. These people also have a well-adjusted ability to drink pints when you meet them of an evening without a demonic history of coke abuse forcing them to leave early for fear of ending the evening talking shit in Kensal Rise with someone they never liked.

❛ The people I used to really hate were the stylists ❜

I didn't manage to strike up such an easy rapport with everyone I had to work with. The people I used to really hate were the stylists. Early on in my career, when there was still a lot of money around in the music industry, a stylist used to materialize pretty much every time I had to do a video, or photo-shoot for *Mixmag*. They'd hold up clothes to me, saying, 'How about this?' And they'd always be some boy-band jeans with the fake wear and tear down the thighs and a T-shirt with a proto Superdry Japanese slogan on it that was all the rage in *Dazed* magazine. I gave up responding in the end. I'd just tell them what I was going to wear and they would just help keep the fluff off what I'd bought in Selfridge's the day before.

We at The Streets called free clothes 'scoops'. On days off we sometimes found ourselves in one of the many plush West End product-placement basements where any self-respecting chart dweller should find themselves invited to pick out free clothes in the hope they might wear them on the cover of magazines. These are places where you are offered Diet Coke by pretty girls in small open-plan offices adorned with Polaroid pictures of celebrities wearing whatever denim or footwear they happen to be marketing. My policy has always been only to take what I will wear on the cover of magazines. That would have endeared me to the fashion gifting world, if it weren't for my band, who always chose to take the poor PR girls for every garment they carried as well as a few in girlfriend sizes. I suspect my name is mud in the world of fashion product placement, just like every Manc or Scouse band's should be.

It was funny how the kinds of suggestions the photo-shoot stylists made evolved. Around the time of the first album they were all about the boy-band look, and I would be like 'No thanks, I'll wear this Fred Perry please, and these Valentino jeans, and those Nike Air Max'. That was how it went along for the first two years. But by the time *A Grand Don't Come For Free* came around, another ritual was starting to establish itself: every time I was doing anything the stylists would turn up bringing bags of what they thought of as 'chav clothes'.

When people see or hear something they don't personally like, it's very easy for them to overestimate the extent to which they understand it. If you're really not into classical music, there's a good chance that it all sounds the same to you. And the same is probably true for dub-step. But if you think it's easy to imitate something just because it all sounds the same to you, you're probably going to end up making an idiot of yourself. That's why the people who do music for adverts tend to mess up when they try and do a drum and bass tune, or moombahton or whatever the new thing happens to be at that particular moment. It probably sounds OK to them, but the kids who actually like it are thinking, 'This is nowhere near — frankly, I'm not convinced' — or words to that effect.

It's the same with fashion. If you're someone with a big pile of *i-d*s and *Harper's Bazaar*s in your Shoreditch flat who looks at me and decides I look like a chav, the chances are you'll have quite a reductive idea of what a chav looks like. So these stylists would be thinking, 'I don't really understand all this chavvy shit, so I'll just bring a load of randomly chavvy-looking clothes.' But the thing about me is, I actually only like very specific brands.

I only ever wore a Burberry shirt once in my career, in the video for 'Let's Push Things Forward', and even that wasn't a proper one with the check that everyone recognizes. My attitude to brands has always been quite contradictory. On the one hand I really understand the power of them. On the other I also realize what a massive con the whole thing is.

❛ I only ever wore a Burberry shirt once in my career ❜

There was a really good series on BBC3 once called *Secrets Of The Super-Brands*. They did a tech one first, exploring how Apple and the other phone companies make their money, and what and where the margins are.

Then there was a fashion one, which was really funny. They went to a place in Italy that made all the designer sunglasses. It was just one big factory, and they had these production lines where they'd say 'OK, we're making Chanel now' and the stamping machine would go *jigga-jigga-jigga* and all the sunglasses would be Chanel. Then they'd do Diesel. There'd be some tiny change or other to the template, the machine would go *jigga-jigga-jigga*, and out would come all the Diesel sunglasses.

The last of the three shows was about how Burberry had become so successful. They went along to the Burberry catwalk show to interview what's-her-name with the big sunglasses from *Vogue* — Anna Wintour — but the guy doing the piece to camera went along dressed entirely in Burberry. He looked completely wrong, like a comedy chav — exactly the opposite of what Burberry wants to be. I like to think he did that as a subtle piece of satire, but I'm not sure. I felt the same way about the stylists who used to bring me huge mounds of Burberry caps and scarves.

The chav thing never really bothered me. I've been lucky to

meet enough people from very different backgrounds who've been into my music not to have any kind of complex about it. The funny thing about it as a term is that no one thinks they're a chav; they're always focusing on someone they think is chavvier than them. That guy who was a criminal and then won the lottery might've been struggling, but I'm sure even he had people in his mind who were further along the chav spectrum than he was.

I think snobbery is a pretty basic human response. Everyone has something they're a snob about — and when I say that word, I mean it both ways: going up as well as down. People who despise City types or rich people in general are just as bad.

When you go to a normal school, like I did, you're a snob about kids that go private. But if you get the kind of job, again like I did, where you come into contact with a wide range of people from contrasting educational backgrounds, you soon realize that there are privately educated twats and state-educated twats, and their twat-hood is something they have in common. Exactly the same thing applies with people who are totally safe. Obviously this is quite an easy thing to say, in an 'Ebony And Ivory' kind of way, but it's true as well.

❛ The look I really liked was late-period football casual ❜

If I was going to retrospectively overcome my snobbish impulses towards stylists and give them a helpful checklist of fashion do's and don'ts for the early stages of The Streets — before I got into my *Miami Vice* phase — I would start off by telling them that I was really into Aquascutum. But in broader terms, the look I really liked was late-period football casual.

I did sometimes wear Fred Perry, but not in a Damon Albarn

vintage retro kind of way. I was more into what you would prob-ably call the Stone Island era. I never actually wore that brand, because that would have been too obvious, but I did like CP Company, which was basically the same firm. They did really nice jackets which I would always wear with dark blue designer jeans and Nike Air Max TNs to mix in a bit of a rap element. I had them in every colour and would get the new ones whenever they came out.

The funny thing about the whole Stone Island thing is that this was the style of clothes that would have been worn by people I had good reason to be wary of back in Birmingham. But once I got to London I didn't have to worry about them any more. I felt liberated. I was free to wear the kind of stuff I would've liked to wear when I was actually being the person The Streets' songs were about, but couldn't because it would probably have got nicked.

Well, maybe not so much the clothes, but definitely the jewellery. Because I'd been robbed so much walking around Birmingham when I was growing up, it was just not possible to have anything on display; T-shirt, jeans and trainers was as far as you could go. But once The Streets was up and running I felt much less exposed, so I could get quite into my jewellery. That was partly something I'd got from my sister, who's always worn quite a lot, and partly something that came from hip-hop.

‘ I went to the estate-agent's on my BMX ’

The vast majority of *A Grand Don't Come For Free* was recorded in Stockwell, in the flat I bought with the advance I got for my publishing. As if to prove that allegations of chav-hood were grotesquely ill-founded, I went to the estate agent's on my BMX.

The office was in Herne Hill, which is in South London, just down the road from Brixton. I parked my bike outside and walked right in, and I remember thinking that the guy didn't seem that impressed. I couldn't really blame him – I probably had my hood up as well, and I'd have definitely been wearing my Nike Air Max TNs (or '120 bubbles' as Kano calls them).

I told him I wanted a flat, and he asked me what I could afford. When I replied 'Maybe four hundred?' he took some pleasure in breaking the news to me that this probably wouldn't be a big enough monthly payment to rent anywhere. Explaining to him that I meant four hundred thousand and I was planning to pay in cash was a bit of a *Wayne's World* moment – 'Oh yes, it will be mine.'

He took me to a series of places which basically all looked the same, then he took me to this development which it turned out he was putting together himself. I'm not sure if he saw me coming, but I do remember that I wrote 'Cunt' on the very last cheque I signed to him, although I'm not entirely sure why.

It was a former pub that got converted into flats. There was quite a weird layout, which I got to have a big say in, on account of buying it off plan and being one of the first people to sign up. I was able to decide all these things that wouldn't normally be down to someone buying their first home, like where the stairs were and what the flooring would be.

6 They weren't floodlit or anything – I'm not Imelda Marcos 9

All the choices I made were based on what would happen if you had a party. You came in through the front doors on to a kind of mezzanine balcony, so the living room was below you and you could address the assembled guests. Generally you'd be returning from the off-licence with a load of cans and would therefore be assured of a warm welcome.

As you walked forward into the flat, the first things you saw were all my trainers, which were laid out on racks. They weren't floodlit or anything — I'm not Imelda Marcos — but there were a lot of them, and it was nice to be in a position to facilitate a suitably upfront mode of storage. On the other side of the living room was a kitchen, and behind that an upstairs bathroom and the spare bedroom, which was sometimes used for that purpose, but more often became a studio.

There was a tiny outside space which essentially ended up being a graveyard for IKEA chairs. I think I had one party in that garden. It wasn't even a place to smoke, because we smoked in the flat. I had this amazing giant brown corner-unit sofa in the main room (I've only just got rid of that, which I must admit I am a bit gutted about, but one of our Polish builders who's just had a kid has taken it, and I'm sure he'll give it a good home).

There was also a huge flat-screen telly which was a present from Warner's after either 'Fit But You Know It' or 'Dry Your Eyes'. The rest of the downstairs was my bedroom and another bathroom. The whole place was quite shonky but also quite unique. The more cynical among you may think it sounds like a high-concept branch of Foot Locker, but I prefer to think of it as more reminiscent of Prada in New York.

Either way, there was this odd thing that was part of the safety requirements which meant you had a fire escape through one of the other flats. Actually it made a lot of sense, because if there had been a fire I'd have been fucked: I was basically in the basement and the main door was upstairs.

The other flat was unoccupied for quite a long time — it seemed not everyone was as instantly enamoured of this development as I had been. Sometimes we'd be really messed up and having this crazy party and we'd just go in there. It felt weird because it was empty, and you were a bit paranoid in case anyone found you in there, but that probably added to the fun. In the end two really nice people moved in, so I stopped using their flat as a warehouse space.

Looking back on it, there was quite a strong *Wayne's World* element to my life as a whole at that time. If you wanted to describe that flat as a young man's wish fulfilment fantasy in 3D, that probably wouldn't be too far off the mark.

The great thing about hip-hop is you're allowed to enjoy the fruits of your success. You don't have to pretend to or even actually feel guilty about it, like indie bands do. That was one of the things I always really admired about Oasis — their refusal to go along with that kind of hypocrisy by implying they were having anything other than the time of their lives.

Your ideals as a person are shaped by whatever scene you are in, or on the periphery of. At the time of the first album, in terms of the people who were buying the records and going to the live shows, The Streets was probably more of an indie thing than a rap thing, but in my mind at least it was very important that it should be presented as part of a broader hip-hop tradition.

Once the second album came along and I started doing stuff with Kano and the Beats and various grime remixes, it got easier to make that explicit. But right from the very beginning I knew that conspicuous consumption wasn't just something that came naturally to me, it was something my musical heritage, not to mention all the people I was hanging out with, actively demanded.

9

For me it was the musical equivalent of the moment in *Being John Malkovich* when John Malkovich goes through the portal into his own brain

Insofar as I had a single personal ambition with regard to my music before it began to become successful, it was probably that I wanted to be there when someone played one of my songs in a club. In the mid-to-late nineties, when I was really into Armand Van Helden and all those early speed-garage tunes, that was definitely what I would have aspired to.

However, once it finally started happening — which would've been around the time of 'Don't Mug Yourself' — I realized very quickly that it was an experience I didn't enjoy at all. I just found it really claustrophobic. For me it was the musical equivalent of the moment in *Being John Malkovich* when John Malkovich goes through the portal into his own brain, and everyone's wearing masks with his face on.

If a DJ played one of my songs when I was in a club now, I'd leave, but before it actually happened it was all I ever wanted. There's a lesson in that somewhere. Maybe I should frame it in a more positive way: I still like the idea of people playing my music in clubs, and I used to think that I wanted to be there when it happened, but now I know I don't. I guess that's what's called personal growth.

When *Original Pirate Material* first came out, I hardly did any interviews. But there was a period a few months later on, after the album got on the Mercury Prize shortlist, when the level of promotional involvement required from me suddenly seemed to go up. I'd only been talking to journalists for a few months, but I'd already had a gutful of it. I just thought it was absolute shit and totally the wrong thing for me to be doing.

I realize nothing comes across more diva-ish than people who make music complaining because other people are interested and want to talk to them about it. But if you're as obsessive about every aspect of the end product of your creative process as I am, you tend to be very resistant to anything that threatens to get in the way.

The main problem with interviews is once you get to the point of doing, say, twenty in a day, you're basically having the same conversation over and over again. After ten hours of that, not only are you repeating yourself to the point of obliviousness, you're also — and even though this seems contradictory, it is actually possible for both of these things to happen at the same time — hyper-aware of every word you're saying. Nothing's natural, you're not really having a conversation any more, you're completely on autopilot.

Obviously this is quite a dangerous state of mind to get into when your job is talking over a load of beats. But that's not even the worst of it. The real problem is that you first got into music because you believed in its capacity to honestly convey ideas and emotions, and now you're just going through the motions. When you find yourself in this situation in your early twenties, you feel like you're being an absolute whore, and at some level you are.

If you have a talent for refining and developing a public persona, you probably learn to ration it out and keep the story moving, but that is quite a difficult knack to reconcile with actually being creative. It's kind of a different thing — more like being in marketing than being an artist.

Don't get me wrong. I'm not saying marketing doesn't have a part to play. People in really big bands think about marketing a lot. When they're in the studio they are generally thinking about making big songs, but the minute they're out of there they're thinking about marketing, because deep down it's all about being a big band, and you don't become a big band without wanting to be one.

As I've got older, my opinions on this issue have softened a bit (though it may well be how few interviews I've agreed to do that's allowed me to take a more balanced approach). I've realized that even though you might feel like you're prostituting yourself by saying the same thing in a series of different situations, the people who care about your music don't necessarily see it that way. Unless they're either in the music industry themselves or a rabid enough fan not to hold you morally responsible for anything you do, the chances are most of them won't see more than one or two of those twenty interviews. So when you say that thing you've said loads of times, they'll probably read it as if you only had that conversation once.

Two important realizations come from this. The first is that the person the decision about whether or not you're going to be a complete tart matters most to is you. The second is not to be too up yourself. There are plenty of different ways to disappear up your own arse once you start to become successful. As if the media in your own country don't offer you enough opportunities, there are also the people who like you abroad to contend with.

Unless you reach the level of true international pop sensation — like, say, Coldplay, or Adele — you're essentially dealing with Anglophiles all around the world. The core of the following you attract will be people who love English culture and probably make a big point of supporting an English football team.

> **' They were Swedish, spoke with cockney accents, and had a strangely reverential attitude to widely feared West Ham hooligan crew the ICF '**

In America, for instance, the first album was quite big on student campuses; the people who came to the live shows once the hipster buzz had started to calm down were the same kind of people (or even the actual ones) who'd have gone to see Blur before me and Arctic Monkeys after me. There's nothing wrong with this at the time — you're really happy to see them, and they're really happy to see you. But any evolutionary theory worth its salt will tell you that when a particular species gets geographically isolated, it will tend to develop exaggerated characteristics.

The same thing that applies to finches in the Galapagos Islands also applies to Scandinavian kids who fetishize everything British. In Sweden, there was this weird sect of really full-on football hooligan . . . I'm not gonna say impersonators, but certainly enthusiasts, who were really into us.

You know those old Jam fans who go to gigs by any new mod band in the desperate hope that they will sound sufficiently like The Jam to help them get over the primal trauma of Paul Weller destroying everything to start The Style Council? They were kind of like them. Except they were Swedish, spoke with cockney accents, and had a strangely reverential attitude to widely feared West Ham hooligan crew the ICF.

They were genial enough people — just enthusiasts really. And when you're twenty-three or twenty-four, as I was at that time, it's hard not to find this sort of thing completely hilarious. We used to get a bit of something similar in Germany as well, but because they had their own teams that were really good, they could focus all their energies on Bayern Munich versus Bayer Leverkusen. I didn't get the impression that there was too much actual fighting going on. It was more about emulating the style of British football hooligans. They were like those Japanese fans who have the whole hip-hop thing down to a level of detail which the rappers themselves wouldn't have the time or the energy for.

There's no harm in giving these kinds of audiences a certain amount of what they want. But if you get too caught up in that process, you're in danger of turning into some kind of international Dick Van Dyke heritage act.

❛ I probably did go to the kebab shop pretty much every day ❜

It's very easy to become a parody of yourself, and the pressures pushing you in that direction don't ease off once you get home from overseas promo trips. When those few interviews I did right at the beginning of my career came out, before the first album was even doing that well, I remember Nick Worthington pulling me aside and saying, 'Turn the geezer stuff down a bit.' I didn't like hearing that at the time, but it was probably a lesson I needed to be taught. The artists who don't learn it are often the ones who don't really get past their first album.

I think there was one specific interview I'd done where they set it up as 'A Day in the Life of a Geezer', and I kind of went along with that, so there was a lot of going to the kebab shop in there. It's a difficult balance to get right. In the long term, people want you to be honest, but when it comes to the particular job they're doing with you, the journalists you're dealing with need something that's going to jump off the page, and the temptation to give it to them is quite hard to resist.

The other problem is, when I look back on my life at that point, I probably did go to the kebab shop pretty much every day. And get blazing drunk more or less every night. I had a pretty clichéd life, to be honest. So maybe it wasn't so much a question of stopping myself descending into self-parody as of drawing a discreet veil over the extent to which that was actually happening.

I realize I've gone on at some length about some of the complications that arise when you first become successful. I've not done that because I think (or have ever thought) that people subject to these complications deserve any sympathy. I was having the time of my life, and the last thing I'd expect anyone to do is feel sorry for me. I just want to try and colour in the background which *A Grand Don't Come For Free* came out of.

❛ Once you have the drama, the song writes itself ❜

It wasn't that I was embarrassed about my new celebrity lifestyle and didn't want to alienate people by writing songs about it. I probably gave that impression when I was trying to explain my motivation at the time, but the fact was my life wasn't all that different when I was making my second album to the way it was when I was making my first. I was just doing the things I was doing in my own flat in Stockwell, rather than in a shared house in Brixton.

The reason I decided to write *A Grand Don't Come For Free* as episodes from a single unfolding narrative was because I'd got so into my songwriting manuals and books by Hollywood screen-writing gurus — not just Robert McKee, but Syd Field and John Truby as well — and I wanted to try and put what I'd learnt from them into practice. Every song needs a drama at the centre of it, and once you have the drama, the song writes itself — that's what I firmly believed, and still do believe. I'm not alone in this conviction, either. It's something pretty much all rappers seem to be sure about.

When you listen to hip-hop, you're kind of enveloped in their awareness of it. These guys are telling stories about killing people, but, with a few highly publicized exceptions, no one's really killing anyone. No one's actually got a gun. They talk as if they have, and they might've seen one in a pub, once, but generally that's as far as it's gone. They may be microphone assassins, but they're not actually murderers.

There's nothing self-conscious about the decision they make to do this. I don't think Dizzee or Raekwon ever tell themselves, 'I'm creating the persona of a man who carries a gun and is willing to kill anyone.' They just know it's what's expected in the musical culture in which they operate — in the same way people have to die horribly in operas.

I was creating drama in the same tradition, but I needed to do it in a way that felt closer to me. I wasn't starting from scratch, but I wanted to do something that was consistent with both the culture my music had grown out of and the person I actually was. I'd always felt like I was a songwriter of some capacity, and I knew I wanted the songs to be exciting, so I decided the best way to ensure they turned out like that was to come up with a fictional story about a character whose life overlapped with my own.

Sometimes that was done in a roundabout manner, but the subject matter of the songs on the album that ended up working the best — 'Fit But You Know It', 'Blinded By The Lights', 'Dry Your Eyes' — was all drawn fairly directly from my own life experiences. That didn't stop them being stories, though. But I think all rap music is, and rock 'n' roll too, come to that. Every now and again something comes along which you think is 'authentic', in the way that 50 Cent was when his first album came out, but if you believe in it too literally, you're liable to get horribly disillusioned.

I'm not saying rap or rock 'n' roll are all lies. You can stumble on moments of honesty that will knock you off your feet. But the closer you get to those moments, the harder it is to escape how much work has gone into them.

❛ It was a bit Nirvana-y, only the other way around ❜

I'm also not saying that the people who make records always have a clear understanding of the effect their words and music are going to have. I'm living proof that this is not the case.

When I made my first album, I wasn't remotely conscious of where it belonged in the market-place. I got it all wrong. I naively thought, 'It's so obvious. Once this comes out, everyone I know will understand it.' Then it didn't really register with the people I thought it was aimed at, and an audience I'd never considered ended up really liking it.

As you get older and more experienced, you begin to covet that kind of innocence. The great thing about *A Grand Don't Come For Free* is that it inadvertently gave me a second bite at that particular cherry. After *Original Pirate Material* I was so convinced there could never be any correlation between the people who liked my stuff and a mass audience that I never bothered trying to court one (if I'd been doing that, I certainly wouldn't have made a concept album about someone losing a thousand pounds down the back of the TV). I just went ahead and did exactly what I wanted, and it miraculously transpired that this was just what the mass audience was waiting for.

By the time 'Fit But You Know It' came out, I was already noticing a big change in the crowds at the live shows. All of a sudden, the people coming to see us were the kinds of audiences I'd always imagined my music reaching. It was a bit Nirvana-y, only the other way around. When Kurt Cobain became really popular, he started hating all his band's new fans, but for me the opposite was the case. I found it much easier to relate to people who only got into The Streets *after* 'Dry Your Eyes'.

‘ *Tupac was never a real gangsta, he went to stage-school* ’

The success of *A Grand Don't Come For Free* made me realize that there's only one way of reaching a certain type of person, and that's by being big. You're just not gonna reach them by any other means.

I know this probably seems like putting the cart before the horse, but actually it's not. The truth is that there's a wider audience which you'll only have a chance of connecting with once you've reached a certain level of recognizability. It makes no difference if what you do is perfectly calculated to appeal to them; if it doesn't come to them through the right channels, they won't notice it.

I was lucky that I'd made such an unconventional debut album and it had done all right, because that gave me the confidence to think that what worked for me was telling it like it was. If I'd been really cynical and that had been successful, I probably would have done that again.

50 Cent is quite guilty of that, I think. He believes that he has a role to play and he plays it in quite a ruthless way. Yet when it first happened, the whole *Get Rich Or Die Tryin'* phenomenon wasn't nearly as cynical as he seemed to think. People were awestruck by this great story, and it was very well-produced, big-sounding music. There's nothing cynical about the process which causes people to be impressed by that — it's human nature. So it was a shame he ended up turning the whole thing into a cartoon.

I think everyone is at risk of doing that, though. It's the Mississippi cotton-picker paradox again — you can't be an actual gangsta and travel the world making great gangsta-rap music. You can take the grimiest guy off the street and give him a micro-phone, and it's more than likely the music will be awful. Maybe Jay-Z was a real gangsta once, but he isn't now. Tupac was never a real gangsta, he went to stage-school, but he hung around with the right people and got the idea. Too well, in the end.

When 50 Cent first came out, the really refreshing thing about him was that he had the honesty of a man with nothing to lose. He used to talk about how much he'd loved Tupac when he was growing up. It didn't matter whether what Tupac was rapping about was literally true in the way that 50 Cent's gangsta scenarios would be, the important thing was that he made amaz-ing music. It's really hard to do that, and the fact that he had that ability was the reason people liked him so much. If the validity or otherwise of Tupac's gangsta credentials was totally immaterial to 50 Cent, it's hard to see what reason anyone else would have to be too bothered about them.

10

I worked at Granada Services, Frankley

Before I started working there in my mid- to late teens, Burger King was always my favourite burger. Is it still? Probably, but it doesn't have quite the same magic as it once did.

You know how something becomes greater than the sum of its parts? When you have actually physically assembled those parts, it is no longer greater than the sum of its parts, it is simply its parts. Once you've found out what all the ingredients are, and you can separate out every single flavour in your mouth, the mystery of the burger is gone. I'm not going to insult your intelligence by wrangling this information into a nostalgic musical analogy, but I do think this would be an appropriate moment to go into a bit more detail about the time I worked at Granada Services, Frankley.

It was between the ages of sixteen and eighteen, while I was technically studying engineering at college. Between occasional educational trips to Sutton Coldfield and being glued to my PC and keyboards literally day and night making songs, I also worked at Burger King two nights a week and all day Saturday, with the odd lapse into full-time during the holidays. It was the Granada Services at Frankley (on the M5, just south of Birmingham) who were paying me, but I worked at Burger King. Although they charged a lot more for their food because they were in the services, that didn't seem to make any difference to the rates of pay.

Because motorway service-stations are, by their very nature, in the middle of nowhere, it was not easy getting to work. There was a little estate that was quite near and a lot of the people who worked in that services were from there, but I wasn't. First I had to get to Longbridge and then there was a (fairly) regular Frankley bus service, so you'd have to hang around waiting for this bus full of people going to work at Burger King and various rival outlets.

Once you got there, it was like doing just about any other job when you're a teenager. I was quite an isolated figure and didn't really socialize with anyone (though I was going out to clubs a lot at that point, so I did sometimes bump into people around Birmingham). If I'd served you while I was working there, you would just have seen a normal, bored-looking, slightly spotty kid.

I've ended up being sacked from pretty much every job I ever worked at. Not in a spectacular way, like Eminem in the video where he spits in the burger. It's just that I've always had my own agenda and it's never really fitted with jobs, so there's been a point in every sphere of employment I've found myself in where people have realized that I'm basically writing a song instead of doing what I'm supposed to be doing.

‘ I'm not Mad Frankie Fraser ’

In this case, the job was half assembling burgers and and half dealing with the public. Dealing with the public meant you made loads more money. Not because you got paid more for being socially adept, but because it was easier to supplement your wages with moments of discreet opportunism. I wouldn't want this to become a recurring theme; a few weeks of low-level larceny on an Australian bouncy castle and this earlier brush with sharp cash-register practice in a fast-food environment were the full extent of my criminal activities. I'm not Mad Frankie Fraser.

Every now and again I'd sell a very large man three Whoppers and two Pepsis, but only ring up for a cheeseburger and one drink. No one expects a receipt at Burger King — at least they didn't back then — so I just didn't bother giving them one. And so long as you can do the adding up in your head and you've moved the straws in front of the till so they can't see what you're ringing up, a small-scale informal employee profit-share scheme is entirely practicable. Basically, it's the same as working for John Lewis, but without the paperwork.

I wouldn't say these practices were endemic, but there was definitely at least one other person who'd had the same idea. I wasn't part of a criminal gang, though — I tried to be smart about it, so I never discussed what I was doing with anyone else. It wasn't hard to keep it to myself as I didn't really have many friends at Burger King anyway.

Most of the people I used to hang around with at the time worked at McDonald's, and they were the absolute worst. When we went out to clubs at the weekend, their wealth was noticeable, whereas my financial situation was more hand to mouth (in a literal sense, as far as the one tab of Ecstasy a night that was generally all I could afford was concerned). I don't know if fast-food sales procedures have changed these days, but anywhere you go where chips are called fries and the box of straws has mysteriously moved in front of the till window, I think you can be fairly sure someone's up to something.

❛ I definitely think my family are a little bit socialist ❜

Mine was a family with well-established moral foundations, and my mum wouldn't have been too impressed if she'd found out what I was up to. In fact, I don't think she'll be too impressed now. Sorry, Mum.

In my defence, I think I had a fairly realistic sense that my offences were small beer in the larger scheme of things. And I wasn't enough of a hypocrite to attempt to vindicate myself by claiming they were somehow justified by Burger King's crimes against the environment.

I didn't feel like I was embarking on a life of crime and would inevitably end up drifting into heroin abuse and having a dog on a string. I'm glad to be able to say that this confidence has proved largely — setting aside the odd dodgy moment fearlessly documented (albeit to somewhat mixed reviews) on my third album — well founded.

In the household I grew up in, there was definitely a prevailing belief in the institutions that had improved the lot of British working people. Burger King would not necessarily have been classed as one of those institutions. My mum cooked a lot of roasts and my dad used to do sausage stew once a week — that was his signature dish as far as I remember. We'd probably have fish and chips once a week, but as they both worked full time, once I got into my teens there was certainly an element of getting a pizza out of the freezer every now and again.

I don't remember my dad as having been specifically Tory or Labour — I didn't actually know which way he voted — but by the late eighties and early nineties even people who might have been sympathetic to Mrs Thatcher early on thought it was going a bit wrong. I think it's a fairly widely held view that every political dream pursued to its end becomes fascism. Factor in the possibility that the NHS might be in danger, and it was no wonder that by the time I was old enough to notice, Labour seemed to be in favour pretty much throughout the nation.

Although hip-hop (Public Enemy excepted) is not often explicitly political, rap's implicit ideology tends towards aspirational conservatism. Obviously there's more to it than 'get trainers, then get money, then keep it', but there's no denying the prevalence of that kind of materialist thinking either. Nor was there any question that this way of looking at the world was slightly at odds with the way my parents would traditionally have seen things.

I definitely think my family are a little bit socialist — in the same way that I think almost everyone in England is. And the reasons why I would view my own culture from this slightly outside perspective come purely from hip-hop. I always had a lot of respect for the way my parents raised me. But whatever the rap thing is, I held that in very high esteem too when I was growing up, and I was very ambitious to be a part of it.

You know how it is when you go into a shop and ask the price of something and it's much more than you expected? Like, 'How much is that shirt?' 'It's two thousand pounds.' I've always been quite good at saying 'Hmm . . . yeah', like I'm even more interested now, rather than gasping and making my astonishment obvious. I can't be certain mine was the first generation of Skinners to have that knack, but I suspect it probably was.

As my career went on, and particularly when the time came to move to New York and make my third album, there was definitely a part of me that started to see something a bit hypo-critical in our innately left-wing society. Even the very appealing adaptation of it which the Scandinavians have come up with. That's a great culture, but it's founded on a delusion. It's not their innate decency that's paying for everything, it's the fact that they've made loads of money out of oil.

Once you live there for any significant period of time, you soon realize that people in America don't see themselves as a country that looks after the rich but where the poor can go to hell. They see themselves as fundamentally attached to freedom, and with freedom comes the government not telling you what to do, people taking responsibility for paying their own health insurance, and hospitals competing to supply healthcare on an open market.

British people don't generally like it when you talk about competing. But competition is why that wine you get in the pub tastes so much nicer now, and you're no longer eating pork pies the barman's wife made two days ago. Meals compete with other meals and in the end the diner wins. I realize that sounds a bit Darwinist, but I do have a basic faith that even a capitalist society will not let too many people fall through the cracks. I know some might consider this faith misguided, and even I'm not quite sure where it comes from. Maybe going to secondary school in an area (Bournville) that was once a model village set up by benevolent Quaker industrialists might have something to do with it.

Either way, at the same time as maintaining my hard-headed, even slightly mercenary, hip-hop-inspired socio-economic attitudes, I always had my enduring, and very English, distrust of obvious showing off to contend with. I'd be exaggerating if I said this ideological struggle was tearing me apart, but it was no wonder having a number one album left me feeling a bit conflicted.

The first time The Streets took me back to Australia, I felt really privileged. I'd met an insane number of people from all over the world when I was in Sydney originally, and I felt like a lot of them weren't going to get to go back there. They probably all had normal jobs by then.

' I guess that was the punchline – there was no guy '

Heading back Down Under wasn't quite what I'd expected, though. I knew the places, but I didn't know the people. Even now it still comes as something of a shock to me when I go there. By the end of that millennium year there were so many people I knew, yet somehow they've all gone.

This seems to back up the suspicion that Australia was my equivalent of university; I've spoken to people who've been back to the town they went to college in and had a very similar feeling. It's humbling to discover that this place was so important to you but you no longer matter to it. And the latest load of people who've just moved in and think the place is all about them are in for a shock when they go back too.

I've already mentioned the bar I worked in where the manager was a terrible coke-head. I won't say its name to save the publisher's legal department any anxiety, but in all my years in the music industry I've never seen a more Jekyll and Hyde coke addict than this guy.

Every now and again you might get cornered after a gig by someone who will bang on at you in a coke-fuelled way about the lighting or whatever their personal interest is, but even when people get really lairy, there's usually an undertow of friendliness to it. This guy wasn't like that, though. We really liked him during the day, but at night he would just berate us. I remember him asking me once what I did away from Australia. I told him I was a producer and he went into this massive rant at me — 'You're not a fucking producer! You're no one! You're just working in a bar!' Obviously there was an element of truth in what he was shouting, but that didn't make it any less evil.

That first time I went back to Sydney, I went back to the bar to try and find him. I actually took a few people along with me. I thought, 'I'm going to find this guy and be, like, "look at me now".' I really wanted to confront him with how wrong he was, so this whole little sub-plot in my life would have a punchline. But it turned out he didn't work there any more. I guess that was the punchline — there was no guy.

‘ I sat there in my track-suit next to a load of people wearing dinner-jackets ’

The ultimate demonstration of my mixed feelings about the public acknowledgement of success was the way I behaved at awards ceremonies. I only ever went to two: when the first album was up for the Mercury (I'd learnt my lesson by the time the second one was nominated and I stayed at home and watched that on TV), and when I won a Brit Award for *A Grand Don't Come For Free*. I found these two exper-iences so painfully embarrassing that I've never really spoken to anyone about them since. But I suppose if I'm ever going to face down those awards-show demons, this is the place to do it.

Dizzee Rascal was up for the very same awards over the years after me, and going to the ceremonies didn't seem to stress him out in the slightest. I wasn't sure why our reactions were so different, but I admired and maybe even envied his capacity not to let it bother him. Maybe his hip-hop mindset was subject to less static interference than mine.

I suppose it's the disdain-for-being-seen-to-be-showing-off thing again that made those kinds of events such a nightmare for me. It's like 'Why the fuck are you there, allowing someone else to tell you what is good and what is bad?' It just doesn't make any sense, unless you subscribe to the idea that other people know more than you about what it is you should like about music.

Obviously the reason bands, or Dizzee come to that, bother to turn up is the hope of selling more records. I want to do that too, so I certainly wouldn't criticize anyone else for openly pursuing that goal. I just didn't seem to be able to do it comfortably myself. At least, not in that arena.

When I went to the Mercurys, I got really really drunk. I sat there in my track-suit next to a load of people wearing dinner-jackets — which is ridiculous in itself. I mean, I've been to black tie events, why not just fucking wear one? It's an occasion. It's not like you're getting into bed with the system.

I've always hated it when bands say, 'Yeah, we'll go, but we'll tell everyone it's a load of shit, and then we'll have a fight.' But essentially I was doing exactly the same thing — slouching around the table in my track-suit, absolutely slaughtered, with everyone who'd worked really hard to help my record do well, and a load of other people who were just in the music industry and wanted to have a nice evening. I can't remember what I said when I had to go up and speak to Jools Holland, but my wobbly impression of the evening as a whole is that my behaviour was pretty horrific. I don't think anyone was impressed with me at all.

❛ If you can't find cocaine at your own record company's party when you've just won a Brit Award, then the music industry really is in trouble ❜

The only other major awards ceremony I turned up at was the Brits, and that was because they wanted me to perform 'Dry Your Eyes'. I've never objected to doing a song on TV in that kind of situation. I don't know why, but it always felt like being on *Top Of The Pops* or *Later* was OK, even though it's just as desperate as turning up at an awards ceremony in some ways.

We did the gig, performed the song, and it seemed to go really well. I think people liked the fact that we didn't make a big production of it and throw loads of money at the staging, which is a mistake you'll often see made at the Brits (though it was fun when So Solid Crew did it). But after that stripped-down success I suddenly thought, 'I can't do this sitting-at-a-table with-the-cameras-watching-me thing,' and I just lost my bottle a bit.

I had a security man at that point, and I just asked him to take me home. He was a proper bodyguard — he'd been doing Chris Martin before me (and I think he's worked for Lily Allen since, which must have presented its own problems). It's not like you think you're Justin Bieber — I'd never have walked around town with security in the daytime — it's just that things get to a level where you have moments that are a bit hairy. Mainly it's at gigs — outside the venue, even getting on the tour-bus — but it can happen anywhere you get concentrations of people who are particularly excited and/or drunk. At those specific moments you need someone there to help you, or you just wouldn't be able to go anywhere.

Anyway, this guy wasn't in the business of arguing with me, so he agreed. And when the time came for me to be presented with the award, I wasn't in the room. Ted had to go up and accept it for me, and he took Beats stalwarts the Mitchell Brothers up with him, which was good, because they were subsequently to be the subject of scandalous neglect by various music industry awards-giving authorities.

Most people probably assumed I was face down in a big vat of drugs in the toilet — which I effectively was, but in the comfort of my own bathroom rather than in the full glare of the media spotlight. It was as simple as that, really. I went home at about nine, then everyone else came back after the Brits was over and we all got really mashed up. There was also an aftershow party hosted by Warner Brothers, and by the time it got to about two in the morning I decided I quite liked the idea of that, if only because I was probably going to be able to get some more drugs there. If you can't find cocaine at your own record company's party when you've just won a Brit Award, then the music industry really is in trouble. But by the time we got there it was really late, and most people had already gone home. I walked in and the few stragglers who remained were all asking, 'Where have you been?'

Then I saw this massive ice-sculpture of the Warner Brothers logo — the shield one they have on Bugs Bunny — and I thought, 'I'm having that, cos I'm sure I've fucking paid for it.' So I picked it up, carried it out of the room, put it in the back of the Range Rover my security man was driving, and we drove it back to Stockwell and put it in my bath.

It lasted three days. I'm not kidding. Those things just don't melt.

III

Crisis: *The Hardest Way To Make An Easy Living*

11

We bought Mum and Dad a place in Barnet

I put some of the money from 'Fit But You Know It' towards help-ing my parents get somewhere to live down in London. The house in Birmingham that my brother and I had grown up in was bought by our old next-door neighbours (I think they wanted a loft conversion and we had one by then, so they just sold their house and bought ours instead of installing their own).

We bought Mum and Dad a place in Barnet, but the week before they were due to move, Dad died. One thing that we all took great comfort from at the time was that he had been really excited about moving — because Barnet was where his sister and all his family were — so it was nice that there was something he was looking forward to right at the end of his life.

The other thing that worked out well was that Mum decided to go ahead with the move. Just a few days after his death, she was gone. At the time this felt a bit weird, because it was like 'Oh, Dad's died, and he's never going to get to move to Barnet', but it turned out to be a really good decision, because Mum didn't have to live on in the same house, and she could make a new start somewhere she knew he would've liked.

Obviously it was a lot of upheaval for Mum in a short space of time, but she coped with it really well. It definitely helped that my brother Dan moved down with her. He hadn't been living at home all that time, he had lived in other places, it was just that thing a lot of people go through in their twenties and thirties, where you move in with someone but then it goes wrong so you come home for a while. He got married recently, so he's untied her apron strings now.

I was living in the party-flat in Stockwell at the time of my dad's death. But a year or so later, after I'd been away in New York, I effectively moved back in with Mum myself. I'd been living with a girl called Laura on and off in Stockwell for a while, and even though we'd broken up, she stayed on in the flat while I was in America (which was great, because I wanted to make sure the place was looked after). So when I finally returned to London, I never went back to South London, I just stayed in Barnet.

Laura was a student — she's a graphic designer now — and the relationship I had with her was at that point the biggest and most serious of my life (and remained so, until I met Claire, who I'm now married to). It had a complicated beginning at a Chemical Brothers concert, around the release of my first album, and it lasted, in a kind of on/off way, for what seemed like a very long time, but was in fact two or three years. She was really important to me throughout that time.

It sounds like a cop-out to say that it ended because my life became incredibly complicated. What I mean by that is not 'it wasn't her, it was me', it's that I think relationships need to be linear. In an ideal world, they start in one place, then get bigger and bigger, and then either end or carry on. Laura and I weren't like that. We were never formally living together, and because I was travelling so much, the time we had together always retained an episodic character. When you're under the kind of huge pressures I was at that time, a relationship probably needs to be more constant than ours was if it's going to survive. And that's one reason why I was quite happy to follow in Dan's footsteps back to my Mum's roasts once I came home from America.

People might think living at your mum's is not a particularly good look for an international pop star, but so long as you don't do it for too long, it works really well. It's not like you don't have the confidence or wherewithal to make your own way in the world. And it's really important to have familiar faces around you when you come back from touring, first because you've got used to being part of a large group of people with a shared sense of purpose, and second because it's good to have someone to remind you that the life you live when you're not on the road needs to have a few more boundaries in it. We had some really good parties at Mum's, but no one was racking out on the kitchen table. (Since someone pointed out to me the other day that the expression 'racking out' is not in universal usage, I should explain for the sake of clarity that it's slang for laying out a line of coke. It's not just a rap or a rock 'n' roll thing, though. You don't have to be involved with either of those two notoriously fast-living activities to know what 'racking out' means. All you have to do is live in Barnet, which is a pretty fun place. In fact, it's a veritable coke cluster.)

> ❛ *Paul Oakenfold sent a blunt to my dressing room once, with a note that said, 'Calm down'* ❜

For me, living part-time at my mum's was like the best of both worlds. On the one hand, I'd get that kind of homely feeling, and on the other there was no need to start getting into arguments with her, because every few weeks I'd be off on tour and then I could do whatever the hell I liked.

Paul Oakenfold sent a blunt to my dressing room once, with a note that said, 'Calm down.' This is a veteran of Primal Scream and the Happy Mondays, so if he's telling you that, you know you've erred on the messy side. We had the same live agent for a while, and we were both playing the Miami dance music convention. I was onstage first, completely annihilated, shouting at all these beautiful American dance fans with dummies — or 'pacifiers', as they call them — stuck in their mouths.

Dance was massive in America even at that time, but still kind of on an underground level. Paul came on after me, being worshipped and doing the whole 'pointing at people in the crowd' thing, like he does. I was basically just staggering around pouring brandy all over people at the side of the stage, and eventually had to be removed by security. It wasn't quite as much of a breach of etiquette as the more celebrated stage invasions of Jarvis Cocker or Brandon Block at the Brits (or Kanye West at the MTV Awards, come to that), but I had certainly crossed a line.

My mum's dad was a sailor in the merchant navy, and he definitely liked a drink. Let's just say he was pretty serious about his rum and leave it at that. By the time I was growing up, he and my gran lived in Birkenhead and we used to visit them fairly often, until they died quite close together when I was in my teens. (I never knew my dad's parents; I don't even know what they did for a living. From the point of view of my generation, it was so long ago that it was probably something I wouldn't even recognize, like being a blacksmith or making barrels.)

As a result of her own experiences growing up, my mum has never been impressed by drinking. She doesn't find it very funny. But her sceptical attitude to the benefits of alcohol never rubbed off on me. Especially when it came to performing live.

> ‘ *I stand by the proposition that getting fucked up is* *honest* ’

Someone who saw me perform a lot in the early/middle stages of The Streets' evolution as a live act once asked me if I thought I had a 'moral obligation' to be so pissed I couldn't really be sure what I was going to do next. I didn't look at it in quite those terms, but my biggest fear about playing live was always that I was going to end up doing the same thing every night, and maybe I did see heavy drinking as a kind of insurance policy against becoming too slick.

I remember doing 'Don't Mug Yourself' on *Top Of The Pops* and being so off my face that it was virtually an out-of-body experience. The strangest thing about my decision to go on live TV in that state is that even though in theory it went against my beliefs, because I do feel it's my job to entertain, I've never regretted it. I didn't feel bad about it at the time, and I don't feel bad about it now. Maybe my value system has room for the idea that someone going on *Top Of The Pops* completely off their face is actually quite entertaining.

People who watched that performance will obviously have made their own judgement as to whether it was entertaining or not, but I do think there's always been a rubber-necking element to British rock 'n' roll. That kind of car-crash thing – where you go to see Pete Doherty in the expectation that he might perhaps get electrocuted – is definitely something that we cherish in our culture. And it was always important to me to leave open the possibility that when I went out onstage everything just might go completely tits up.

There are disadvantages to getting fucked up on a regular basis when you're touring. And one of them is that the night after having a really good show, you'll often have a really bad one, because you're still dealing with how fucked up you were the day before. Obviously that's a shame, because a crowd who've paid to see you have as much right to see you at your best as any other.

Then again, what people want (or what they say they want) is something where they can genuinely feel, 'This only happened in Liverpool — Manchester didn't get it.' Of course there are risks attached, but I still feel both sides of the human equation — performer and audience — are being truer to themselves and each other if they aim for that. Even if it goes horribly wrong, I still think it's way better than that grimly ritualized 'Good evening, Liverpool!' kind of thing.

It's hard to hang on to your illusions when you're on the festival circuit. I've seen a lot of bands who don't just play the same set every night, they also say the same things between songs, and in that context I stand by the proposition that getting fucked up is honest.

From a personal point of view, it only takes about four days before that cycle of alternating between really crazy shows and really grumpy ones starts to get to you. So you definitely can't do it for ever. But I do think that the moment you stop being like that, you've lost something, a particular kind of honesty which you can never get back. I still think of those shows as having a tremendous degree of merit, because there was an un-predictability about them that was palpable.

There were probably only a couple of nights where it went totally Joe Cock-eyed. One weekend in Amsterdam when I totally lost it ended up being the starting point for the third album. As if that's not a sufficiently permanent record of the kind of state I got myself into, the whole thing was also preserved for future generations on video.

Dizzee was on before me, and I'd fallen asleep in a drunken stupor under the stage. By some fluke, my subconscious woke me up during his encore. I didn't really know where I was, but by the time they'd sorted out the changeover I'd somehow found my way upstairs to the stage. Then someone handed me my microphone. I was just spinning around and lying on my back and being completely incoherent. I remember wandering round the festival afterwards and people just telling me, 'That was absolutely awful.' The Dutch didn't really get it, and I couldn't blame them. I don't think the British would have got it either.

> ❛ It was just before alcopops came in, so we had
> 20/20 and K cider ❜

I've often found it strange that when performers discuss their relationships with drugs and/or alcohol, the time after they became successful tends to be taken in isolation. The fact is that patterns of consumption are probably established in your formative years; what happens once you're in the public eye just builds on that foundation.

In my case, there was nothing particularly exceptional about my teenage drinking antics. It was the same kind of thing anyone from my generation, or any generation, might have got up to. I was fairly heavily involved in park-bench drinking from quite an early age. It was just before alcopops came in, so we had 20/20 and K cider — proper teenage park-bench stuff — alongside really suspect weed that may or may not have been oregano.

It wasn't one specific park, it could have been any green space to the south of Birmingham, depending on which mate's parents' house I was staying at. I had friends in Stirchley and Harborne, so they were the two main places. Stirchley is more working men's clubs and snooker, which was a good option, because you could join a club at sixteen, and that was quite a discreet way to drink pints until you'd be literally falling over.

The one on the Pershore Road in Stirchley, opposite the bowling alley, was where we had the most success in pursuit of that goal. Whoever looks the oldest goes and gets the pints, and the rest of you sit in the corner and hope no one chucks you out. I certainly wouldn't have been the one who looked the oldest. And, riddled with epileptic anxiety as I was, fronting the age thing was not a knack I had fully acquired.

Luckily, the large gentlemen on the doors of Birmingham's city-centre nightclubs were not too fussy about the exact birth-dates of the long lines of kids queuing to gain admission to their establishments. I don't know why they'd want to let me (or any other sixteen-year-old, really) into their nightclub, but the funny thing is that when they do you think they really believe you're eighteen. It's actually like 'Mate, we don't believe you're eighteen, we just want your money', even though you haven't actually got any. It can't just be about what they make off the door — I've always assumed the dealers must have to pay their way as well.

' It's getting in, then drugs, and from then on you're drinking tap-water out of a bottle '

House music came hand in hand with Ecstasy — that was just kind of what you did. Much the same as it is today, except I think in the mid-nineties Ecstasy felt like it was more directly associated with clubbing — or maybe not even clubbing itself, just club-type people — whereas I've noticed recently that it seems to have become increasingly ubiquitous. Even though apparently overall drug consumption is actually going down. Maybe that's why, though — because Ecstasy use has lost its proper focus.

When I was young, people might occasionally drop one in a pub to muck around, but that was seen as quite a weird thing to do. Now those students who can still afford it will do it anywhere. It's just part of a night out, and doesn't really have anything to do with music. Then again, I suppose once I started doing Ecstasy on my travels on tour, listening to music wasn't really that big a part of it. People in glass tour-buses shouldn't throw stones.

I know slightly younger, Fabric-type people who did Ecstasy for the first time to drum and bass. So there's a generation of kids, probably about five years after me, who think Ecstasy and drum and bass go together perfectly. Maybe that's more of a London thing — once I'd moved down to the capital, I kind of lost contact with Birmingham — and as weird as it seems to me, it makes total sense to them.

It's all about what's around when you first start going out, I suppose. The ages of sixteen and seventeen — that's the time in your life when everything seems really exciting and new, and you're probably always going to look back on it as the apex of youth culture, whatever people who were young in the sixties, seventies, eighties or nineties (or the noughties, come to that) try to tell you.

The combination of house music and Ecstasy was certainly pretty hard to beat as far as I was concerned. We're talking about a drug which causes a chemical change in your brain to make you feel intensely happy, and it is logical that this is a good idea. Even though the level of Ecstasy consumption I was able to afford as a teenager would seem laughably healthy to the hardened consumer of later years. Half a tablet once or twice a week — we're talking about £1.75 worth to get you through to the morning here. When you're sixteen and you go to clubs, you've got no money — you're literally walking home. Before that it's getting in, then drugs, and from then on you're drinking tap-water out of a bottle.

The idea of buying an alcoholic beverage in that environment seemed impossibly decadent and luxurious to anyone not in possession of a full-time job. And the high price of beer was not without its compensations. There are other motivations for going out to clubs beyond music and drugs, and a measure of sobriety can be a useful asset to young men on the lookout for female company. After all, as I believe it says in a song (and I promise this is the only time in this book I am going to quote my own lyrics as if they were handed down on tablets of stone rather than as a basis for further discussion), 'Those who are hammered don't get to nail.'

❛ Ecstasy is awful in Australia ❜

I think what tends to happen when you're a teenager is you do Ecstasy pretty much every weekend and it's really great. Then after a while — maybe a year — you start to see how it's affecting your life and your mood, and you get a bit bored and give it up for a while. Not for good, because that Ecstasy button will always be there to be pressed for the rest of your life, but certainly for long enough to get into something else, whether that something else is going to the gym or getting drunk in the bars you're now old enough not to have to worry about getting thrown out of.

Obviously a fair amount of settling down into routines goes on. But once I was working full-time on Broad Street — when I was eighteen/nineteen, just before I went to Australia — I remember combining that 5.30-p.m.-on-the-dot-Thursday-and-then-Friday people-with-jobs canal-side bar culture with casting my net a bit wider in search of places where you could hear alternative forms of dance music. There were definitely some university drum and bass nights that I went to after The Institute got closed down because of all the gun-play and the nutty stuff, and break-beat was quite studenty as well. Just because I had a job, that didn't disqualify me from seeking out more eclectic places to get pissed in.

This was the going-out frame of mind I was in by the time I got to Sydney. And it was a good job, too, because Ecstasy is awful in Australia (at least, it was at that time). Not to mention really expensive. I think the average price there in 1999/2000 was something like thirty quid a pill, so I hardly did any drugs of any kind while I was Down Under.

It was all about schooners of Toohey's, or VB (Victoria Bitter), which is a bit rank. My favourite was probably Crown, which is quite a rich premium lager that comes in a weird-shaped brown bottle. It's a bit like Red Stripe, but kind of the opposite, because Red Stripe is what you get at grimy raves, whereas Crown would be bracketed more with the fancy Mexican beers which come straight out of the fridge by the bar. Either way, you probably wouldn't have more than three of them before you moved on to shorts.

12

I know plenty of people who smoked brown and were fine — I suppose I'm one of them

I've done a lot of drinking in my time, but I've never liked vodka in my Bloody Mary. I'll quite happily have a Virgin Mary and then get really pissed on vodka afterwards. I like the way that drink's name celebrates the purity of not containing any alcohol, but at the same time it sounds really dirty, as if that's just the way the Holy Ghost likes her.

The divide between innocence and not innocence is often more blurry than it first appears. Anyone looking at someone in the music industry who'd indulged fairly extravagantly in drink and drugs — not at Premiership level, but certainly Championship with a good cup run — might assume that person had taken a few early steps on to the slippery slope, and then fame's gravitational force had pulled them downwards at an ever-increasing rate. I'm sure that's the way it is for some people, but it wasn't that way for me.

I still remember how shocked a lot of Londoners were by the way my first single mentioned tooting rocks and smoking brown as if those practices were no big thing. The fact is, in Birmingham at the very end of the last century, that's exactly what they were — a normal part of life.

I've mentioned already how seductive some people in my home city found the transition from smoking draw to smoking smack — it just seemed nicer and more effective. If you smoke draw regularly enough that it becomes a habit, that will cost you a certain amount of money, at which point smoking a bit of brown can very easily start to look like it's giving you a bit more bang for your buck. The dangerous thing is, once you're looking at the decision on an economic basis, you're only one step away from thinking, 'I could be a lot more efficient about this if I inject the heroin rather than smoke it.' At that moment, two apparently straightforward and rational financial calculations have potentially landed you in a lot of trouble. I think something as simple as people's desire to make their money go further informs a lot of drug-related decisions which have traditionally been viewed in a more apocalyptic light. Having to watch your finances can be beneficial too, though. It definitely kept me off cocaine when I was a teenager in Birmingham.

There was a fair bit of coke around at the house clubs I used to go to in the city centre. I don't think it was a gay thing — the gay contingent would be more inclined to do ketamine, or whatever else the new drug might be. It was more an anyone-who's-got-a-full-time-job thing. But even once I was in full-time employment, I could never really afford to buy any for myself.

Coke certainly wasn't going to help me buy that laptop or sampler I was working towards, and it always seemed like not very good value for money. The few experiences I had with it were quite fleeting; they all seemed not to last very long and yet still manage to put me in a really bad mood (a combination of consequences which I can now say with some authority doesn't really change once you can afford to buy your own).

As a basic rule of thumb, I would tell anyone planning to embark on a career of non-life-endangering recreational drug consumption that as long as you stay away from smack and crack you'll probably be fine. I smoked a bit of the latter around the time of the first album, and it wasn't much fun at all. Then again, I know plenty of people who smoked brown and were fine — I suppose I'm one of them.

❛ Obviously weed-fumes are something of an occupational hazard in hip-hop ❜

In a reversal of the traditional narcotics pecking order, the one I had to watch out for was weed. That was the only drug that ever caused me to have a fit. When you're an epileptic, drug-taking is very much a matter of trial and hopefully not too many errors. People used to be surprised that I could get away with taking Ecstasy amid the flashing strobe-lights of a house club, but I wasn't totally reckless. If doing Ecstasy had given me a seizure once, I don't think I'd have done it again.

When it comes to chemically induced abandon, it's a question of feeling your way to what you're OK with. I think it happened twice that smoking weed gave me fits. It was at the time when I was making a lot of beats in our loft in Birmingham for rappers who would come to my house and we'd get really stoned together. I can't remember exactly what happened on those two occasions, but I'm pretty sure it wasn't good, and as a consequence I've never been much of a smoker since.

Obviously weed-fumes are something of an occupational hazard in hip-hop. And I did a couple of sessions with grime MCs later on when the amount of pharmaceutical grade Mary Jane being consumed was just completely nutty. It's a miracle any of those people ever got anything done. If that was alcohol, they'd be like madmen drinking meths on the street.

I always liked to go out and get fucked up, but I never drank or did any drugs in the studio. If I was working, I wouldn't touch a thing. Partly because I took the music too seriously; but I suppose some people would say that the studio was the biggest drug of all. It didn't feel like that, though, it just felt like work that had to be done. And once I'd finished whatever I was doing, I'd call a few people and we'd be off out, sometimes for days on end.

❛ When you step inside that life, it's just the same as the one you were living before, only slightly amplified ❜

There's a reason I've made so much of the wilder aspects of the life I lived between my second and third albums not being new to me. And that's to establish the context for the one thing that really was. The success of *A Grand Don't Come For Free* did initiate a single massive shift in my psychological outlook. That huge change was the realization that life was never going to be any different. Ever.

When you're on the ascent, you're an outsider looking in, and you see all of this fun that's being had, and all of this great music that's being performed, and you imagine that if you could only be part of creating that thing which people appreciate so much, then you could totally transform your life. You start down that path and people begin to get into what you're doing, and then it gets bigger and bigger, and finally it gets kind of as big as it can be, and at that point you realize you're actually no different to the person you were at the beginning.

It's such a ridiculous cliché to say this — even now, seeing it written down makes me uneasy. Which is why I'd never have talked about feeling that way in an interview at the time, because you know if you even touch on it, that's the thing the paper or magazine will definitely run with, and it'll just be really boring for everyone. But that awareness doesn't change the fact that when you experience this revelation for the first time, you really want to tell the world.

As much as you know that this is the last thing anyone wants from someone who has just become successful, you feel this incredible desire to educate people. To show them that however good it looks in all these dreams you have, all these magazines that you read, when you step inside that life, it's just the same as the one you were living before, only slightly amplified — with free clothes, more fake tan and better cars.

I'm not saying that extra amplification doesn't have any impact, because it does. For some people I'm sure it drowns out (at least for a while) the noise from the voices in their head. But for me, it just made them louder. You reach a point where all the things that you thought would go along with what you were doing actually have come along. You have as much access to them as you're ever going to have, there's nothing you wanted that's not attainable to you, yet you still feel incredibly insecure. You're convinced that whatever it is you're working on is a complete pile of shit.

It was some time yet before the release of my third album — at which point Britain's rock critics would do their best to confirm me in this uncomfortable suspicion. In the meantime, my face suddenly seemed to be looking back at me from the side of every bus in Britain.

I'd signed up to feature in this big ad campaign Reebok were running — 50 Cent and Jay-Z were part of it as well (although if they found the additional exposure as unnerving as I did, they did a much better job of hiding it). I could hardly complain about the loss of privacy entailed in my face being plastered all over the nation's billboards, because I'd been quite happy to take Reebok's money. But as more and more of the giant posters went up, I decided to move to the US.

> *6 Once your face is on bus-shelters, you get this really dramatic ramp-up in terms of the number of people in the street who recognize you 9*

In a short space of time I'd gone from being fairly cool to really quite commercial. Obviously there was nothing new about this transition in terms of pop history. But it was still new to me. It wasn't that I had indie-snob scruples about reaching a more main-stream audience — quite the reverse, as I've already explained — but some of the consequences of my new-found public visibility did make me a bit uncomfortable.

My second album had reached that level of success where you're kind of on the minds of people in general, but once your face is on bus-shelters, you get this really dramatic ramp-up in terms of the number of people in the street who recognize you. Apart from anything else, it's no longer a surprise to them to see you in that setting, because they've got used to staring at you while they wait for the bus.

It all actually dies down pretty quickly. The minute the campaign's over and posters of someone else's face go up over yours, the heat will be off. As soon as you're not there, it'll all be OK again. But at the time you don't realize how quickly every-thing's going to go back to normal, and it feels like you've bought a one-way ticket to somewhere you didn't necessarily want to go.

I couldn't say I hadn't actively pursued this newly heightened profile. I didn't put up too much resistance when my manager, Tim Vigon, came onboard after my first single and said, 'Right, at the moment this is just a dance thing, which is all wrong. You're not just a producer, you're an artist, and you shouldn't just be doing vinyl releases with Locked On, you need to be on the cover of the *NME* and getting reviewed in Q.' From that point on, this was pretty much how we went about things – straight down the middle, in the industry's eyes – even though it wasn't really where I was coming from.

Whatever else you might think about this plan, there was no denying it worked. The fact that I was taking quite a conventional path in career terms seemed to reassure people who might otherwise have found my music a bit too idiosyncratic.

When 'Has It Come To This?' originally came out, it'd seemed quite alien and dancey. The first few times it got played on The Dreem Team's Sunday morning UK garage show on Radio 1, some people told me afterwards they couldn't tell if I was white or black. But by the time I'd won a Brit Award for *A Grand Don't Come For Free*, I'd essentially become the British rapper who was popular enough that Q journalists who really preferred Blur, Madness and The Kinks had to at least pretend that they liked me.

I was perfectly happy with this favourable consensus of opinion at the time, and I don't look back on it with any regret now. But in retrospect, one thing is certain about a position like this: it can never last.

13

I was fully living the dream

I'd always wanted to learn about rap music from the place where rap music was made, and I had some good friends who worked at my American label. So once the billboards with my face on started going up all across the UK, New York seemed the obvious place to escape to.

When I first got there, I lived in Mid-town for a while — which means north of Times Square but south of Central Park (48th Street, I think it was). Then after a few weeks I moved down to the Rivington Hotel on the Lower East Side. It was a really nice hotel, I could get room-service whenever I wanted, and there was a McDonald's just round the corner. I was fully living the dream. Even though it was strange being on my own, all sorts of crazy things were happening, and I was writing songs about them as I went along for my new album. It was great.

What I wanted to do was see rap music happening in its natural habitat. By that I didn't mean so much the places where it had started — Brooklyn or the South Bronx — as the corporate board-rooms in which hip-hop's character was increasingly being defined by the early twenty-first century. I asked Craig Kallman, my contact at Atlantic (which was the company Vice records was releasing my album through), to introduce me to Puff Daddy's old A&R guy at Atlantic.

Atlantic weren't quite running things to the extent that Island/Def Jam were, but they had Missy Elliott and a lot of the Dirty South people. So I took this guy to a basketball game (I was still well in with Reebok, so they could sort me out really good tickets). He didn't know who I was at that point, because I'd not been that big in America, but after we went to the game together he was willing to let me sit in on some of his meetings.

The best one was the R. Kelly/Sean Paul A&R conference. There's this office at Atlantic with a projection screen at one end of it, so you have Craig and all his colleagues sitting around the table in New York, and at the far end the table goes off into a screen, which is LA. It was fascinating. They were all talking about the beat, and the chorus, and how they needed a 'street record'. Then this guy called 'Hip-Hop', who's quite famous and used to be at Jay-Z's label Roc-a-Fella, joined in with the meeting on his mobile phone, because he was stuck in traffic.

You have to be very confident in your own abilities to go by the name of the genre you're working in (I've always felt that way about Bob Rock as well, who produced some of the slower Metallica albums). And the perspicacity of Hip-Hop's contributions to the debate did nothing to suggest a high level of confidence wasn't entirely warranted in his case.

I felt so privileged just to have met some of those people and witnessed these processes at first hand. I came away from it feeling that the way they were going about their business was a lot more honest than what's often perceived to be the more artistically respectable way of approaching such decisions. I've never liked that singer-songwriter mentality, where you write the first load of shit that comes into your head and then go, 'That's the song, because that's what I wrote at this one moment, and only by keeping it exactly as it was can we maintain a spiritual connection to that moment.' I've always thought that is absolute bollocks.

I think it's a hip-hop thing, really (as well as a Hip-Hop thing) — the idea that you can go, 'The verse is really good, but we need a new chorus', and then call up someone who does choruses and they'll come up with one. I've always identified with that way of doing things, which is why there's always been such a large element of chopping and changing in my own recording process. The only real difference is that in Hip-Hop's world there are lots of different people involved, whereas in my case, all those meetings happen inside my head.

‘ *I was just as star-struck meeting Puff Daddy's keyboard player* ’

Once you've done a few festivals, you've met every band. You've spoken to Oasis and Blur and the Beastie Boys. But much as I enjoyed encountering all those people, I was never really star-struck in the way I was when meeting Jay-Z or Kanye West. That's not a reflection on the relative charisma levels of the individuals involved, more of the quest I was on to get to the heart of that hidden culture which makes one record sound so much better than all the others.

I've never found myself talking to someone in a rock band and thinking, 'I've got no idea how you've done it.' When I met Noel Gallagher, he was lovely, but I didn't spend hours beforehand wondering, 'How is it that Oasis have achieved greatness?' To me it was always obvious how they did it (which is not to say I or anyone else could do it in the same way): great songs, played on a 335 Gibson turned up loud, and recorded really well. That's it. The simplicity is part of the appeal.

But when it comes to working out how (for example) Erick Sermon gave those Redman records that impossible sound which no British hip-hop tune ever got close to, that's an altogether more complicated and mysterious equation. There's just this thing which has happened in the studio that I'm totally in awe of, and every aspect of it fascinates me. I was just as star-struck meeting Puff Daddy's keyboard player (who is an amazing musician and R&B singer in his own right, to be fair) as I was meeting Puff Daddy himself. Maybe even more so.

Because apart from signing Biggie and Mary J. Blige — which were obviously good moves — and generally being a great A&R man, it was always clear in terms of Puff Daddy's pop career that it wasn't necessarily all about the music. Why else would he have made a record that sampled Sting? That's what you need to have to be Puff Daddy — a willingness to sample Sting, and do that video, and go on that awards show. When you meet his keyboard player, on the other hand, the music is definitely what it's all about. And the same applies to talking to Big Bass Brian, who mastered all of the Dre and Eminem stuff.

‘ He had the Gucci trainers on, which I'm a big fan of, but they weren't box-fresh ’

But the great thing is that when you see the rap recording process underway on home turf, it makes it more attainable. You realize that this music is not created on other planets by magical super-beings, it's the work of real people doing essentially the same thing as you.

When you see an indie star on the front of the *NME*, they've usually got that kind of dirty look about them, but because the picture has been taken by a good photographer, it still looks good. When you see them in the flesh, though — the indie stars, not the photographers — you realize that actually they're just dirty.

Rappers' standards of personal grooming are generally much higher. But they're never quite as pristine when you meet them as they look on album covers. Those Dipset records are ridiculous for that — the artwork's all fur-coats, purple Range Rovers and hundred grand necklaces, so when you see them dressed in anything less, it comes as a bit of a shock.

The same thing happened with Puff Daddy. He had the Gucci trainers on, which I'm a big fan of, but they weren't box-fresh. I know this is ridiculous, but I do remember thinking, 'They're not brand new, he's just a normal guy.' The trainers weren't totally scuffed, but they must've been at least a few weeks old. He might have been slightly unshaven as well. Fair enough, he was only in his studio — they were doing the Biggie Smalls duets album at the time — and he did have his SUV out the front, and there were some security guys buzzing around, but he wasn't dressed up in any way. It was like getting a peek behind the screen at the real Wizard of Oz.

A few days later, the screen was properly back in place again. I went to see Kanye West at the Madison Square Garden Theater, which is the smaller of the two venues there, as he was doing a warm-up show for a big tour. Puff Daddy (or P. Diddy as he was probably known by that time) came to that gig too, and this time he was fully suited and booted. He processed through the theatre and everyone was screaming for him and it was very much like 'OK, that's P. Diddy'.

He probably just walked straight out the side-door and went

backstage, but it's satisfying to see someone be — not just do, be — exactly what you expect of them. I realized that all these guys are basically just trying to make another song that works, but because they're Americans, they also have to put on a show. We don't really have that. We just have indie people in dirty trainers and knackered old jeans. I guess that's why, when the time came to do the artwork for my third album, I went for the Rolls-Royce and the *Miami Vice* look. I was just trying to bring back a bit of mystique.

❛ *It was mainly the rich landowners who wanted independence* ❜

They say you shouldn't meet your heroes, but I'm glad I've met some of mine, because it made me more idealistic, not less. I realized that if you're serious about trying to get that sound which is better than everyone else's, you cannot afford to have any limits. What hip-hop in the late nineties was all about was making sure everything was done to a very high level in a state-of-the-art analogue studio facility. So when I was in New York, that process was always the main thing I was paying attention to — I was looking at the desk, what microphones they were using . . .

People might find it strange that the record I made on the back of all these detailed observations was *The Hardest Way To Make An Easy Living*. Of all the accusations people levelled at that album — and there were many — I don't think anyone said it was a slavish tribute to rap studio-craft. But what I was trying to do was come up with my own response to the honesty I'd heard in the hip-hop recording process. It was how impressed I was by how smoothly all the different parts of that machine worked together that made me so determined to do everything on my own.

The relationship between US and UK hip-hop has tended to be seen as a fairly straightforward reversal of the one that caused the American war of independence, with them as the colonial masters and us valiantly trying to forge our own cultural identity. But it would probably be truer to say that the musical relationship mirrors the complexities of the earlier imperial connection.

Americans have been educated to think that we taxed them too heavily and they rose up as one saying, 'We're not gonna take this from you tyrants — we want liberation!' Therefore England is evil and America is brave and free. But what actually happened, at least in the early stages, was that it was mainly the rich landowners who wanted independence, and they only hyped up the revolutionary rhetoric to put a gloss on their own self-interest.

I don't know how I ended up reading *Empire* by Niall Ferguson. I didn't realize that he was a global hate-figure who is widely viewed as the Jeremy Clarkson of history, but even if I had, it wouldn't have stopped me really fucking loving the American stuff in that book. The way he dissects how the East India Company mutated into British colonial interests is interesting as well.

If you look at places like Ghana or the Ivory Coast, it's pretty hard to make an argument that the British Empire was good for them. Even as I was reading I was thinking, 'This is a bit controversial. What he basically seems to be saying is "They were lucky to have us, because we gave them roads".' But once you get to America, his whole argument starts to hang together much more effectively. Because when you look at the whole Tea Party thing (the original one in the eighteenth century, not the wonky Sarah Palin reboot), that was all about people who'd done pretty well out of imperial trading networks deciding that they wanted a bit more political independence so they wouldn't have to pay so much tax on all the money they were making.

I'm not drawing a direct analogy between the way I recorded *The Hardest Way To Make An Easy Living* and the people in Boston throwing all those big boxes of tea into the river Charles (though if sampled correctly, the splash might've made a nice rhythm track). That would be ridiculous.

What I am saying is that hip-hop is fundamentally American. And if you take away America from hip-hop, you're basically left with Africa. That's kind of what grime is. It's amazing how many of those British rappers who've stopped the idea of a British rapper being a contradiction in terms — Dizzee, Kano, Lethal Bizzle — have got Ghanaian or Nigerian parents. Whereas traditionally, British black music — and you could definitely see this with the earlier generation of garage MCs, and the drum and bass guys before them — has been dominated by people from Jamaican backgrounds.

But if you're neither American nor African — if you're a white guy from Birmingham, say — and you still want to make records that are part of the same tradition as the music Big Bass Brian masters, you're going to have to work really hard at putting your own personal stamp on them. In my case, a lot of creative effort was put into exploring my ambivalent attitude towards hip-hop's traditional propensity for outward display. On the one hand I was irresistibly drawn to it. On the other it wasn't quite me. I think the psychological backdrop to the renting-a-Ferrari-in-Vegas story without which no showbiz memoir is complete will probably provide the requisite illumination here.

'It was totally cannibalized by the end, which made me quite angry'

My dad was really into cars, and the rest of the family was too. We used to go to classic auto shows at the Billing Aquadrome. I always really enjoyed that when I was twelve or thirteen, because my dad would teach me to drive by letting me manoeuvre his car (which would have been a Montego or Sierra, vehicles that may themselves one day attain classic status) around the field.

My cousins all had motorbikes, which they also used to ride around the shows too. I used to really want one of those, but something just got in the way ... I suppose all my money was going in one direction, and I was too focused on my music to be thinking about life on the open road. My brother had no such distractions, though, and he was madly into it.

He had a knackered old VW Beetle, which my dad eventually bought off him and gave to me for my seventeenth birthday. It was left in the garage for a while, because I couldn't have lessons while I was still having epileptic fits (I couldn't have afforded them anyway, because I was saving all my Burger King money for studio equipment and occasional trips to The Steering Wheel). My brother put the money towards buying another Beetle for himself — a pink one, which was actually really out of character for him — and then proceeded to remove all the bits from mine that his needed. It was totally cannibalized by the end, which made me quite angry.

At that point in my life I definitely imagined myself as someone who would eventually learn to drive, and I think if I'd stayed in Birmingham I would have. You've got to have a car there really. The nature of the public transport system requires it.

Once I'd got to London, though, there wasn't really any need. I had about three lessons when I was twenty-six, but I never really got into it. Wiley bought a Bentley once, but he left it outside somewhere in East London and it got nicked. Which is another reason why I think that kind of Alan Sugar or Simon Cowell in-the-back-of-a-Rolls-Royce-Phantom vibe is still probably the best way to go if you're determined to make an impression.

When you're in your late teens, a car is a status thing. It's a way of saying, 'Look at me, I'm old enough to drive', and that's part of what motivates most people to learn. But if by some quirk you push through that barrier and come out the other side in your mid-twenties, people know that you're old enough to own a car by then, it just so happens that you don't.

The random nature of that life-choice is never more pleasurably apparent than when you're driving a Ferrari around Las Vegas. We rented it in Ted's name and then I drove it — I knew I could drive, because my dad had taught me. The whole experience was just really fun. The car was a red 355, which was my favourite Ferrari until the 458 came out (even though you're not owning them yourself, that's no reason not to maintain an interest).

We went out to Death Valley and put it through its paces. We weren't drunk or doing drugs — it wasn't like *The Hangover*. There has always been an element with me of staying up for days on end and then thinking, 'This is getting annoying', and giving everything up for two weeks. That kind of ebb and flow has always persisted with me, even at my most indulgent. It was never the full Pete Doherty.

I don't even think I've really got an addictive personality. I'm obsessed with making music, and everything else is subordinate to that. I do get into things at a very high level, but because I have such a short attention span when it comes to anything that isn't making songs, I go off them very quickly. I have the happy knack of being able to do something potentially quite reckless, what 99 per cent of people would consider way too much, and then get bored of it and stop straight away.

That's especially true with drugs. There are certain people out there who are hell-bent on destroying themselves from the start. Whether it's something that's happened to them in their childhood, or just some mental condition in their brain, encoded in their synapses or whatever, you feel like they've always had that urge, and heroin or cocaine enable them to scratch that itch with fatal efficiency. I'm really lucky not to have that impulse. I've just got some kind of thermostat inside that clicks me off.

14

The final amount as far as Warner's were concerned was probably nearer a million

In the early stages of The Streets, Ted Mayhem was my inter-national promotions person, which meant he was responsible for coordinating all my various campaigns outside the UK, and mak-ing sure things that needed to happen actually were happening. Whenever I went anywhere abroad, from my first album onwards, he would always be there. And since I did a lot of travelling at that point, we spent a lot of time hanging around in hotels together.

He was a good person to have on the team while I underwent my baptism of fire at the hands of the global hipster community. Ted is a total London snob. He has that inverse sense of aspiration that leads him to think dressing smartly equals some kind of plain, boring, northern pride in self-image. His brand of shambolic is every bit as vain as my love of Gucci. Every vehicle he has owned has at some point featured that sticker the council puts on cars suspected of having been abandoned.

What draws me to him is a shared love of genuinely creative action — things that fly at a tangent to all lines of convention.

While I go around playing the carefree geezer about Fabric, Ted actually enjoys driving down to the edge of the Sahara in a vehicle clearly not fit for purpose. He could have been on Scott's exploratory mission to the Antarctic if he hadn't been born into the rave generation and channelled his mental fortitude into purposefully ordering the weirdest choice on any restaurant menu he encounters. He also knows how to book a private jet at short notice, which I think may one day come in handy. All of which is a roundabout way of explaining why when I was planning to start my own record label, The Beats, Ted seemed like the obvious person to ask, so he kind of left Warner's but also carried on working for them through the imprint that we ran together.

Setting up my own label had been one of my biggest ambitions when I was in my late teens. But then my youthful dreams were trampled by the Prince's Trust. And once The Streets got signed I realized, 'What I do is make music — why would I want to be taking on all that hassle myself when that's the label's job?' So the idea went on the back-burner for a while. But then you reach a point where you start thinking, 'Maybe this is actually a way of making more music — by overseeing other people's records and getting someone else to do all the admin.'

The fact that Warner's put up the cash so I didn't have to risk any of my own was just the icing on the cake. I think the way I described the financing of The Beats in the title track of *The Hardest Way To Make An Easy Living* probably led people to believe that it was my £250,000 that was getting spent, but actually it didn't cost me a penny. And the final amount as far as Warner's were concerned was probably nearer a million. I think they were right to give it a go though. I'm sure they've wasted seven-figure sums on projects with less chance of success.

They don't just give you the money. What happens is they agree to release a certain amount of music — maybe three albums a year, something like that — and then they agree to market it. We didn't spend much on recording, because I just did that myself, but once you get into making videos and other forms of promotional activity, the bills really start to mount up.

In retrospect, I think a lot of what we achieved was valid. Two out of the three acts we signed — Example and Professor Green — went on to be really massive afterwards, and a hit-rate of 66 per cent would be regarded as more than acceptable (not to say miraculous) within the major label A&R fraternity as a whole. It's not too late for a Mitchell Brothers revival either. Their police harassment single 'Routine Check' was probably the best thing The Beats ever released.

Looking back on it, I think the problem was just that the music wasn't right for the time. Even though I'd broken through as this weird thing that had somehow got across to more people than the industry had expected, it was still very much a case of 'Yeah, but we don't need anything else like that, because the niche is full now'.

❛ For me, spread-betting was a way to finally experience the joy of sport ❜

Running in parallel with my valiant attempt to redistribute as much of Warner's money as possible to such worthy causes as The Mitchell Brothers' wardrobe budget and Example's development as a lyricist was a second potentially ruinous financial initiative. And this time I was spending my own money.

For me, spread-betting was a way to finally experience the joy of sport. This was something I'd never really understood. My manager Tim Vigon is a big-time poker-player, and a lot of my friends are really into it as well, but it's not a game that has ever appealed to me. I am a competitive person, but sport in general is something I've never fully been able to connect with, for reasons I will now attempt to explain.

I support Birmingham City, and I'll never not support them. Yet ultimately I'm looking at a completely fluid concept of what Birmingham City is, at least in terms of manager, ownership and players on the pitch. I realize that some footballing connoisseurs might argue that complete fluidity is one goal Birmingham City can be relied upon never to attain, but that's not the point. The point is that Tim Vigon supports Manchester United.

He's not a glory-hunter. I do believe he has always supported Manchester United and was happy to do so even many years ago when they were shit. But now his underlying belief in the genius of individuals means that he can quite happily go and watch Wayne Rooney — an Everton supporter from birth who was offered tens of thousands of pounds a week to leave the club he'd grown up at and play for one of the biggest teams in the world and said 'Yes' — and consider that Wayne has somehow become the soul of Manchester United. That's why I can't relate to football, because the nature of its tribalism is fundamentally inconsistent.

> ❛ *Your losses, like your winnings, are potentially pretty much infinite* ❜

I get the idea of stoic adherence to a localized ideal of loyalty, and I get the idea of generalized meritocratic reverence. What I don't get is how those two principles can co-exist simultaneously.

Spread-betting, on the other hand, where you identify a range of likely outcomes rather than a specific one, offers a model of fluidity that does make sense to me. It's more flexible than normal betting, but it's also much riskier, because it's not just a single stake you're putting on the line. Your losses, like your winnings, are potentially pretty much infinite.

To understand how this chance-based leisure activity could have appealed to me so much that I spent several hundred thousand pounds on it, you've got to tune into the mindset I was in at the time. I don't feel very comfortable admitting this, but I think that in the middle of The Streets I got a bit confused about the nature of the project I was engaged in.

Looking back now, I can see that I've spent my whole adult life, and much of my adolescence, making songs that either haven't seen the light of day, or when they have done haven't been particularly popular. In that same twenty-year period I've also come up with maybe two or three tunes that have managed to become part of the fabric of society for a while. This definitely applies to 'Fit But You Know It' and 'Dry Your Eyes', but maybe also to 'Blinded By The Lights', if I'm lucky.

Given that these three songs had come along in such quick succession, I could probably be forgiven for having thought that this new paradigm was henceforth going to be the rule rather than the exception. But the psychological ramifications of that inaccurate prediction would be quite drastic.

I think that to try and align creativity with economics in any way is basically impossible. All of my creative friends have at some point in their careers experienced a meeting of those two concepts which has caused them great problems.

It happens in a lot of different ways. At its simplest, it could involve a band making an album purely for money, but in a lot of more complicated cases it comes down to how you value your time. Most people, even if only subconsciously, put a monetary value on their time. At the most basic level, this might mean that if you work at Burger King, your time is worth six quid an hour (or perhaps a little more, if you've moved the straws in front of the till).

As we move through life, what generally happens — although in quite an uneven, slapdash way — is that your time is gradually worth more as you climb the ladder in whatever field of expertise your ladder happens to be planted. In the course of most people's lives, they'll probably be able to tell you fairly accurately what their time is worth at any particular moment. But when you write songs for a living, you have to come to terms with the fact that there are no parameters for how much your time might be worth. For a very high percentage of your existence, it will be worth absolutely nothing. But for a very tiny percentage, it could at this time in my life be worth absolutely anything.

What this means is that, in financial terms at least, you have to leave behind the physics of the universe most other people live in. I know it probably sounds a bit over-dramatic, but once you realize you're outside that realm of normality, it really does feel as overwhelmingly big and important as a universe. And apart from the death of my dad, I would say that this was the thing I struggled with most.

You develop a new perception of your working life, which is that what you're effectively doing in the very different universe which you and the very small number of other people in the same situation as you now inhabit is playing poker (not, as I've mentioned, a game I've ever really enjoyed). You're sat at a poker table, playing endless hands. Most of them — thousands over the years — you lose, but then you win a couple.

When you're a songwriter, the thing that will have the biggest impact on your world is whether you write — say, for the sake of argument — 'Dry Your Eyes'. However much you might've thought about what doing this would mean to you over the ten years of losing hands that led up to it, the consequences will still go far beyond what you expected. It's not even so much directly about the money the song makes, it's more about where the song takes you. The repercussions ripple on for years.

❛ It's like the last decade versus all of human existence on this planet ❜

It did take me quite a long time to write that song: if I add it all up, taking away any day when I wasn't working on it at all, it was probably about a month. But compared to the time spent on all the other songs I've written that weren't 'Dry Your Eyes', that is nothing. It's like the last decade versus all of human existence on this planet. And yet it led to such a big change in my economic and spiritual status. ('Spiritual' is probably the wrong word for what I want to say . . . I mean something that refers to the impact it had on other people's emotions, rather than my own.)

Since I've finally come to terms with this aspect of my situation, I can look at any new act coming through — and there are lots of good ones — and know that whether or not they end up writing that song which will take their life down a completely different path is entirely a matter of luck. Once you know that, you realize that every single thing you do is a gamble. And since being creative costs money — apart from anything else, there are studios and music videos to be paid for — to go from that revelation to putting sixty grand on the chance that a particular Ghanaian footballer will be the first to score or the first to foul, or how many red cards there will be for Valencia, it's like, you might as well. You really might as well.

If I went outside now, withdrew a million pounds from my bank account and then went and burnt it like the KLF did, who's to say that wouldn't help my career? Even if I burnt a million quid and no one saw it and it didn't get picked up by the media and it didn't help my albums sell, the disappointment occasioned by this turn of events could still inspire me to write a bigger song than 'Dry Your Eyes'. In that (admittedly somewhat unlikely) eventuality, the whole burning-a-million-pounds initiative could still be considered a success.

❛ At that point, you may as well just play blackjack ❜

Once you get into this mentality, it's very difficult to get out of it. Looking back now, I can see that I was in the grip of a strange paradox — knowing that things were always going to be the same, and never going to be the same, at the same time.

On the one hand you've achieved all you've ever wanted; on the other, you've lost the hope of a different and better life that wishing you could achieve that goal used to give you. And now you've got to try and do the whole thing again without that extra edge your innocence of how little difference it was going to make used to give you.

That's why I've never really regretted the spread-betting. It was probably as effective a way as any of coming to terms with the randomness of my new situation. And all the money I lost, I could just as easily have lost in other ways — you can drop as much as I did (I didn't keep exact records, but it was definitely well into six figures) just by cancelling a tour. And besides, if you let yourself be guided by money, you end up doing all sorts of stupid things.

I'm not going to say spread-betting was a good idea. It wasn't. If only because the only thing it taught me about was spread-betting itself — knowledge which was of no further use to me once I'd decided to give it up.

I didn't know anyone else who was into it. It was an entirely solitary pursuit, based on two internet trading sites which I won't name because I've given them enough business already. I had a Windows mobile, so I was able to place bets on my phone. If it had still been a matter of going into a shop with a load of slightly drunk men pissing their wages up the wall, I don't think I would ever have got involved.

In that sense, the randomness of the whole thing was further emphasized by the chronological precision of it. If I'd had my biggest hit three or four years earlier, the technology that enabled me to squander such a large proportion of the proceeds from the privacy of my own hotel room would not yet have been available.

It is quite amazing though, how consumed you can get by La Liga or the African Cup of Nations, even when you're not that into football. The reason I wrote a song about betting on cricket rather than football was because that was probably the ultimate example of me wagering large sums of money on the outcome of sporting events I knew literally nothing about.

I only did that a few times, but it is a dangerous feeling — when you see the results and you don't even know if you've won or lost because you don't have the first idea how the game is actually played. At that point, you may as well just play blackjack. At least then you understand what it means when they turn the cards over.

I don't really see it as an addiction. I was just at a point in my life where nothing seemed to mean anything, and gambling was the perfect representation of that. The fact that I could lose all this money doing such an insane thing and it didn't even really matter dramatized my situation beautifully. In a way, I think I was almost trying to make myself feel something. But from that point of view, the spread-betting experiment was not a success.

I was never either totally gutted or massively happy about the biggest losses and occasional wins — certainly not nearly as happy as making music has made me. The great thing about music is that every song you do could be amazing. As I've got older I've realized that it usually isn't, but I've never made a song I've not genuinely loved the sound of at the time I was putting it together.

That feeling doesn't linger as long as it used to. The moment I leave the studio now I'll generally be thinking, 'Actually, it's probably not that good, but I did enjoy making it.' But this change is not a bad thing, it's the inevitable consequence of getting a bit older and having a bit more perspective on things. It's not that all bets are off, just that the stakes aren't quite so high.

Looking back on my spread-betting indulgences, I now see them as both a curious pursuit and an expression of my curiosity — like a Victorian folly, or a footballer's racing stables. Luckily for me, there was a point at which I lost that curiosity, and at that moment the whole profligate enterprise instantly became irrelevant.

15

With anti-heroes — film noir-type people — you think of them as being bad guys, but they're always better than their surroundings

I think *Original Pirate Material* and *A Grand Don't Come For Free* had generated quite a lot of goodwill towards the impression of my personality that people got from those albums, and as a result they were happy for me to be living the dream in real life. So when I made a record which basically seemed to involve admitting that I was being a bit of a wanker, and suggesting that in my position other people might easily make the same mistake, it registered with them as a bit of a slap in the face.

I didn't mean it that way. I was just trying to keep my side of the bargain I'd made, to be honest with everyone. But I think perhaps the boundaries I was operating within had shifted further away than I realized from what was considered to be normal. The fact that I was taken aback by how shocking some people found the behaviour I was describing certainly suggested as much.

We all like to think that we're inherently good people, but if you put kids in front of a bowl of sweets with no adults there, they'll steal sweets. If you put kids in front of a bowl of sweets with a mirror behind it, they'll still steal sweets, but not quite so many, because they can see themselves.

Mirrors are not always a force for temperance in the music industry. So the moral of this story for those in my profession is probably this: if you're in a situation where you can do pretty much whatever you want, without anyone calling you to account for it, it's probably a good idea to compare your view of yourself with other people's now and again.

Everyone operates within the confines prescribed by their own particular circumstances. But when you're on a tour-bus in your early to mid-twenties and you're essentially the bread-winner for a fairly healthy business operation, there aren't too many lines you're not allowed to cross. Hotel rooms will get repaired. If you're in one place and the show is in another, someone will generally find you and put you where you need to be.

It's easy to be critical from the outside of the kind of things that go on, but it's hard to be sure you wouldn't go the same way if you were in that position. It requires an immense amount of effort not to, and most people just aren't that disciplined. Especially people whose role in life is to give everyone else the vicarious thrill of knowing what it would be like to live without restrictions.

Someone like Liam Gallagher might project the aura of a badly behaved maverick, but within the realm of his own existence — as an entertainer who makes a living as a badly behaved maverick — he is actually as well behaved as any of us. He might smash up the odd bathroom, but he knows he can afford to pay for it. Obviously it's not nice for the person who has to clear up afterwards, but there's always someone ready to write the cheque, and ultimately Liam makes everyone a lot of money by being this unruly character. It's expected of him; I think people would be disappointed if he didn't do it. I'm not saying it's his duty, but it's certainly his job.

It all comes down to what Robert McKee calls 'the circle of justification'. He wasn't specifically talking about Liam Gallagher when he came up with that phrase, but he might as well have been. The heart of the matter is that with anti-heroes — film noir-type people — you think of them as being bad guys, but they're always better than their surroundings. If you think of the character Humphrey Bogart plays in *Casablanca*, he's a bit of a dude, but he's surrounded by shit and that's what makes him a hero.

If you're making up a story, there has to be a circle of justification that you put your protagonist in. That's why Holocaust films do so well at the Oscars, because the scale of evil involved is so great that it establishes the circle of justification not only for the hero but also for the members of the academy when they're deciding which film to vote for.

As far as *The Hardest Way To Make An Easy Living* was concerned, the circle of justification I hoped to create was that my willingness to be honest about the distance I'd travelled from a conventional moral framework would somehow make the trip worthwhile. This circle worked for me, but that didn't necessarily mean it was going to work for anyone else. As if to hammer this

❛ *You don't actually want to be that person any more, you end up wanting to be the exact opposite* ❜

point home, I was walking through Regent's Park thinking about it the other day when it came to me that what McKee talks about is not the circle of justification, it's the frame of justification, which I personally don't think sounds nearly as good.

In terms of my embrace of the kind of Dionysian behaviour patterns I can't claim to have invented because countless bands before and since have had recourse to them, I think there were two main elements to it. One was the physical — going to Vegas and driving a Ferrari and staying up for days gambling on the African Cup of Nations. The other was more psychological, and related to my perception of my own career.

There was definitely an element of wanting to break with the expectations I'd established. In the music business, once you've given people a clear idea of the kind of performer and person you are, everything becomes very reductive. The story that is repeated endlessly is basically whatever you put in the press biog at the beginning of each campaign, and that transfers over into the ideas pretty much everyone you come into contact with has about you. They're all based on the few words you wrote down on a piece of paper and gave to your press officer in the run-up to your album coming out.

That bit of paper which you give to them becomes what you are.

It's quite fun to play around with this when you're first getting used to it, but if you've got as short an attention span as I have, the idea of doing this same thing over and over again becomes quite overpowering. To the point where you don't actually want to be that person any more, you end up wanting to be the exact opposite. Which is why every now and again you'll see Liam Gallagher on Alan Carr's sofa talking about how he's given up drink and drugs and all he wants to do is stay at home with his wife and kids.

In my case, this process took me in a rather different direction. As I was getting older, I was realizing that people aren't always what they make out. I felt like I was learning things about human nature — as you do in your mid-twenties. You discover that becoming an adult is a bit of a cover-up. You're still young and probably just as bad as you always were, but you develop these kind of airs and graces. *The Hardest Way To Make An Easy Living* was meant to be an attack on the hypocrisy inherent in that process.

Picking up the *Guardian* and being told that I was the bastard Brit-rap love-child of Dostoevsky and Samuel Pepys probably fed into that as well. Because I was so obsessed with the idea of story, you'd think I'd have taken great satisfaction from all these people saying that *A Grand Don't Come For Free* was such an amazing narrative construction. The only problem was, I knew it wasn't, really. Some of the songs were good, but it certainly wouldn't have made a great film.

The frame of justification was not entirely cynical, but I'd certainly ticked the boxes in quite a school-literature-essay type of way. Basically it was a pretty straightforward fairy-tale, in terms of the main character feeling he'd been wronged by the world and then deciding he just had to get back out there and accept things. The more high-flown the claims people made for that album, the more I felt it was just something quite simple that happened to work. I wanted to be a bit more sophisticated than that, and I think I was quite down on humanity at the time, so the right thing to do next seemed to be to describe in forensic detail all the things that weren't Disney about me.

❛ Politicians work to the numbers, and I was doing the opposite of that ❜

It wasn't quite on the level Oasis had with *Be Here Now*, but after the success of *A Grand Don't Come For Free* there was certainly a bit of bravado among the people around me that *The Hardest Way To Make An Easy Living* was going to be a really, really big album. There was definitely an element of masochism in my response to that cocksure presentiment. I just didn't think life should be so easy. I felt a strong impulse to go back to the way things were at the start of The Streets — to pull everything apart and put it back together again.

I know there is nothing on earth more inherently boring than a pop star complaining that no one understands them any more. But given that vast areas of our culture now seem to be taken up with the projection of various different ideals of success, I thought it would be a valid exercise to be honest about the darker reality that lies behind some of those ideals.

Politicians work to the numbers, and I was doing the opposite of that. I was entertaining ideas that were clearly unpopular in the climate of the time, such as saying that it doesn't matter how great your life is in theory, if you've got no reason to do anything but stay up for days doing drugs, then something about your state of mind is not entirely as it should be. This may not be that interesting a conclusion, but it's definitely honest. If everyone else in Britain had been through the same experiences I had, then my third album would probably have been a massive hit.

I don't regret what happened instead. I'd already made two records about things everyone else in the country could relate to (well, not quite everyone, but sometimes it felt that way), and now I was happy to have done something different.

In years to come, quite a few famous people would tell me how much they liked *The Hardest Way To Make An Easy Living*. Some of them would even quote their favourite lines out loud and tell me how much those lines meant to them. But only in private. And unfortunately you can't sustain a career by releasing music that only resonates with celebrities. Even Rufus Wainwright hasn't quite managed to do that.

❛ It was not Rachel Stevens ❜

When you're doing your first album, there are three questions you're obsessed with getting answered in the affirmative. Does this sound good? Is it saying what I wanted it to say? Would I like it if I heard it? That's why first albums are often really good — because you're so totally focused on pursuing those goals.

I was lucky that I managed to retain that attitude with my second album, by the simple expedient of completely shutting out the outside world and ignoring everything that wasn't directly associated with the music I was trying to make. But the longer you go on, the harder it is to do that. And because I'd managed to sidestep the inevitable distancing effect that success brings when I was making my second album, once I got to the third one the change in my situation hit me all the harder. As time goes on, you can't help but think about what you're doing in a more detached way, which is a really bad thing to do.

I don't think it's as simple as saying, 'You've had twenty-one years to write your first album, but you only get six months to write every one that comes after that.' It's more that when you're working on your first record, you're stretching every bit of the knowledge and ability you have to do something you're not absolutely sure you're capable of. But once you know you can do it, you're then dealing with a pre-existing template which you have to redefine in one way or another. Not only is that situation inherently more reactive, you're also trying to stretch yourself in the hope of recapturing the feeling of excitement you had first time round.

You set yourself challenges and develop theories and stratagems, some of which can work really well, but all of which make it more likely that you'll end up being led by the idea of what you're doing, rather than the actual thing. I still think *The Hardest Way To Make An Easy Living* was a really good idea, and I had all this confidence that if I just stayed true to that vision, it would all come out OK. The success of my first two albums had created its own logic, and I was determined to follow that logic to the end, however bitter and twisted that end might seem.

It's good to stay true to your own vision. Even, or maybe especially, when that vision is that you know your life is going substantially off the rails, and you're determined to try to present that situation in an honest way. But because I'd lost contact with that person who hadn't made a record yet, I wasn't really approaching the songs from a point of view of 'Would I listen to this?' Whereas with *Original Pirate Material*, I was just making music that I wanted to hear, and there's not really any substitute for that.

There were only two aspects of the criticism *The Hardest Way To Make An Easy Living* received that I found hurtful. The first was the idea that it was rushed, and the second that it was done under some kind of pressure from my record label. That album was not rushed. It took two full years, in which time — in creative terms at least — I didn't really do anything else. And surely it's obvious by now that if I'd bothered to consult with the good people at 679, there was no way they'd have wanted me to alienate a substantial majority of my mainstream audience by going on a kamikaze mission of truth.

Because to me at the time (and even now) that's exactly what that record was (and is) — the absolute truth of what it was like to be me at that point in my life. The thing about the absolute truth is, it's not pretty, and not everyone is interested in it. But it's still the truth.

In commemoration of that warts 'n' all agenda, I would like to take this opportunity to discuss the identity of the mystery crack-taking pop star who makes a cameo appearance in 'When You Wasn't Famous'. Now that a few years have passed, I feel a point has been reached where there would be no indiscretion involved in revealing that it was not Rachel Stevens.

IV

Progressive Complications: *Everything Is Borrowed*

16

I was never anything more than an outpatient

When it comes to ways of coping with depression, I'm not really British and I'm not really American. I don't think you should just go to the pub and get on with it, which is kind of the classic British approach. But neither do I think that constantly talking about your problems on TV while taking anxious sips from a glass of water is the right way to go. File my strategy somewhere in the middle-ground between Oprah Winfrey and Alf Garnett.

Even at my worst, I was never anything more than an out-patient. And that wasn't in rehab. It was with a really good psychiatrist called Mike McPhillips. He's got a practice in Chelsea where he diagnoses and prescribes treatments, and he's had a lot of experience with celebrity types' unique potential for self-destruction. Once you find out that the person you're talking to has treated Amy Winehouse, you feel quite relaxed about the fact that nothing you're going to come up with is likely to shock him.

There are certain quirks that tend to go with being someone in the public eye. There should probably be a Greek name for the condition of chronic anxiety caused by everyone knowing who you are (but 'peterandrephobia' doesn't have quite the right ring to it). The way mine first manifested itself was quite simply that I couldn't do anything. I was living in a really tiny flat at the time, and I just got kind of stuck in this one room.

When I first started going out with Claire — who's my wife now, as the gypsy Papa Lazarou from *The League Of Gentlemen* would say — I'd not been back from America for long, so I was basically living at home in Barnet. She needed somewhere to stay at the time, so she rented this small place in Notting Hill, which left us with a choice of either moving in there or being at my mum's.

We went for the grown-up option, which meant starting our life together in this tiny, tiny flat above a reggae club that Damon Albarn used to drink in. The place was fine when we went to see it, but very noisy at night. We'd be watching telly thinking, 'Who's making all that racket outside?' Then we'd look out of the window and it always seemed to be Damon Albarn — he really likes to let people know he's there when he's out and about of an evening. The other big local landmark was the laundrette over the road, which people always said was the one in the film *My Beautiful Laundrette* (although I subsequently found out that is actually in Wandsworth).

Claire was still working at Warner's at the time, so she would go out at eight in the morning and I would be left alone in this flat. I might go out and get a coffee, but essentially I would just sit there on my laptop all day. At that time I was doing loads of stuff for The Beats — mixing the first Example album, the Mitchell Brothers' second, and some Professor Green stuff — as well as being in the middle of promoting my third album, and starting work on my fourth.

It was a stage in my life when going outside had become a bit of a hassle. Not at a Justin Bieber level, but just to a point where you know that if you do leave the house, you're almost certainly going to have a conversation with someone you don't know. It's not that the idea of speaking to people is especially horrible, it's just that it increases the temptation not to go out, and if you give in to that temptation too many days in a row you end up going a bit mad.

What basically happened was I lost the ability to sleep. I'd be really tired and I'd fall asleep easily, but then within about twenty minutes my body would wake me up. It got worse and worse over quite a short period of time, to a point where I was actually going crazy.

It felt physical rather than mental, though. I never felt sorry for myself, or overwhelmed by the desire to become a psychiatric patient. There was just this strange thing going on that meant my body wasn't letting me sleep.

> ‘ *It was childish, the sort of thing you've always dreamed of doing . . . and I did do it* ’

Anyone who's listened to *The Hardest Way To Make An Easy Living* could be forgiven for assuming this situation was drink- or drug-related. And in a way, it was, but perhaps not in the way you'd think. At this point in my life, as I'll explain in a couple of pages' time, the problem wasn't an excess of drink and drugs, it was the lack of them.

By the time my third album had come out, all of the really bonkers drugs stuff—the crazy partying nights when I'd be up for so long that when I closed my eyes I would see a swarm of bees — was pretty much behind me. Those waking dreams never really bothered me, because I knew where they came from. They were simply the result of being up for three days and doing twenty Ecstasy, or a hell of a lot of coke.

As you get older, it does generally default to being coke, because people – at least people in the circles I moved in – feel like that's a bit cooler. I don't know why. I think maybe it's just a suburban thing, because I've had much better nights on pills.

I certainly didn't go to many showbiz parties, apart from my own – though admittedly those were pretty good. And there was touring as well. I remember one time in Manchester, we were just up for days, and met all sorts of characters who came in and then went out. I had this massive apartment with a big kitchen, and whenever I finished a drink I would just throw the glass against the cupboards in the corner of the room.

It was childish, the sort of thing you've always dreamed of doing (at least, I have), and I did do it. People thought it was hilarious. Well, I don't think the cleaner thought it was hilarious, but everyone else did.

After the third album there were a lot of questions I needed to ask myself, and also a number of fairly hideous comedown experiences to be gone through. But when that happens you always know what the cause of it is, so you just go to bed until it stops. You feel pretty bad, but when that swarm of bees is surrounding you in a borderline sleep hallucination (and I'm not using that example randomly, it was quite a common occurrence) at least you know it's your own fault.

❛ That's what good managers do – they make you go to rehab, even if you say, 'No, no, no' ❜

Once I was relatively sober but just not able to get myself to sleep, the situation was much harder to cope with, because it no longer had an obvious cause. I'm really grateful that my management made me seek help so quickly at that point. Tim was very straightforward about it: he just told me it was something I needed to do. That's what good managers do — they make you go to rehab, even if you say, 'No, no, no.'

Mike McPhillips spelled the whole thing out for me very clearly. He just said, 'You have chronic anxiety. It's so bad that we're going to have to knock you out.' He told me Valium wouldn't work because it wasn't strong enough, so they put me on anti-depressants. I never thought it would come to that — I'd always felt that if it did, that would basically be the end of my life, because taking them would make it impossible for me to make music — but they weren't being used as anti-depressants, they were being used as sleeping-tablets.

Now I've seen that written down, I realize it would be quite a clever thing to say to make someone who was reluctant to take them feel better about doing so. But it definitely wasn't a full course. And certain anti-depressants do apparently just help you to sleep if you only take them for a fortnight. They worked too — I was out like a light straight away — and they took me off them after two weeks, before the broader range of anti-depressant characteristics could kick in.

❛ I'd been training for the New York marathon as well, and that hadn't exactly been helping ❜

That was a weird time though. It was chronic, in both the traditional English senses, though not the one Snoop would use. But at least I wasn't getting the e-bees any more. Instead I remember spending my time watching loads of documentaries about bands, to try and relax while reminding myself of what was important.

I'd been training for the New York marathon as well, and that hadn't exactly been helping. P. Diddy had been advising me, and he went on to complete the course in something like four hours and nineteen minutes, which is a pretty serious time for someone who it turned out hadn't done it before. So you can see how competitive he was (and is).

Despite all the time I'd spent talking a big game with all the big guns in P. Diddy's studio, I had to back out of the race because the being-asleep-for-two-weeks thing and the running-a-marathon thing didn't really mesh together too well. On my blog I said I'd injured my leg. I can't guarantee that this is the only time I have knowingly told a lie via an online portal. It's not a medium of communication in which untruths are generally acceptable, but 'I can't run the New York marathon because I'm having a bit of a nervous breakdown' would definitely constitute over-sharing as far as I'm concerned (though Kanye would probably think nothing of it).

6 *Essentially what CBT comes down to is that you need to get rid of the 'shoulds' in your internal monologue* 9

At that point — once the anti-depressant sleeping draught had done its job and the immediate threat of having to cross the Atlantic in order to run twenty-six miles had receded — the moment had come (on Mike McPhillips' advice) to go and see a cognitive behaviour therapist. Those are the ones you break down in tears in front of about your deceased father and go into all these strange . . . they're not even Freudian by-ways, it's more like a kind of Buddhism. Not technically — there's no sitting under trees or reincarnation involved — but it does feel like Buddhism, because the essence of cognitive behaviour therapy is stopping yourself from trying to control stuff.

CBT had helped my dad an incredible amount when he was a bit all over the place. He'd got the counselling on the NHS and it really worked for him. So a few years later, when the shit was hitting the fan for me, I was more than happy to give it a try. It's not silly, it's very effective, and the numbers speak for themselves in terms of the success rate.

The cause of the incredible stress I'd put myself under was basically just working too much and following the same downward path on a daily basis. Essentially what CBT comes down to is that you need to get rid of the 'shoulds' in your internal monologue. It's pretty basic stuff, really, but the framework is an amazing principle which just gently reprogrammes your mental cycles into accepting that you can't change the world, and that the only thing you need to be able to control is your reactions to situations you're familiar with. Once you've got that sorted, you're able to take everything down about 30 per cent, to a level which is survivable on a day-to-day basis.

This was the first time in my life I realized that it wasn't possible for me to be working every minute of the day. What had happened when I was living in Stockwell was I'd felt like every minute of the day was work, but what was actually going on was I was working really hard till about Thursday. Then someone would call me and say, 'Let's go out and get fucked up.' I never went to West End clubs. We'd more likely go to a pub in Streatham or Croydon and get absolutely slaughtered, then on to the garage night at Pal's and get some pills. I'd lie in bed all the next day because I couldn't function, get back to making 'Dry Your Eyes' on Saturday morning, do that for a while, then on Saturday afternoon go to the Dogstar in Brixton or some pub in town.

Next thing I knew it would be Sunday morning and I'd go off and have a full English somewhere, before going back to work on Monday.

What I was doing wasn't helping my liver, but psychologically I was quite balanced. I was working hard, but I also had this social life that was just brimming over. By the time I was training for the New York marathon and living in Notting Hill, the really nutty stuff was in the past. There were still big nights out, but it had slowed down a lot. And for weeks on end I was just sitting at my computer screen while Claire went to work.

That's why I still insist that my psychic deterioration was down to a lack of drink and drugs as much as anything else. As bad as those things might be for your long-term health, they're still down-time, which someone who gets as caught up in his own head when he's working as I do desperately needs. Once you settle down a bit, you have to replace the time spent chasing girls or getting drunk in bars with something else, and I neglected to do that.

❛ *For those who are lucky enough to make it into their twenty-ninth year, I do think there's definitely a transition that we go through* ❜

I used to worry about the possibility that I might be an alcoholic. And you could probably make a case for my overall intake having been in line with that concern. But it was never a question of getting up in the morning and needing to start the day with a drink. There were always interludes — periods of frantic activity and then spells of relative abstinence (it was the same with girls, before I met Claire). And besides, someone can be just as emotionally dependent on having a couple of pints of Guinness once a week as on forty-eight Bacardi Breezers. (I'm not going to extend this beverage-based metaphor into the carnal realm, for fear of where it might lead us.)

I think I got out of the quasi-alcoholic routine at just the right time. My drinking was probably at its peak at around twenty-seven, the age at which Kurt Cobain and pretty much all the other famous dead rock stars (including Amy Winehouse) met their ends — because I remember thinking, 'Oh, so this is how that happens.'

I never actually thought I was going to die, but anyone can, can't they? And if I was going to, that would've definitely been the time. It's rarely a genuine surprise when someone in the music industry dies. But there's a kind of political correctness that dictates how everyone is supposed to respond. PC definitely rules the meme, which is why everyone who dies becomes a genius, and you can't say anything bad about them because it's all so tragic. It might be better if people were allowed to be a bit more honest at that point, though, because people who have (either effectively or actually) killed themselves don't really make very good role models.

For those of us who are lucky enough to make it into our twenty-ninth year, I do think there's definitely a transition that we go through. Maybe it's because subconsciously you know your thirties are coming, and you've also had a lot of practice at being in your twenties, but this is the time when a lot of people go, 'Wow, this is getting a bit ridiculous' and start to tone down the partying a bit.

I think when you tour a lot, or you have toured throughout your twenties, you don't need to go out at the weekend to try and get into trouble. Trouble is what you spend most of your time trying to stay out of; you've got a deficit of normality to make up, rather than a deficit of craziness.

This mathematical undercurrent also feeds into one of the great masculine rites of passage. What I mean to say by that is, there's definitely a direct proportional link between the extent to which you think your freedom is going to be restricted by married life and how mad your stag do is. Mine was lovely, but quite boring, which was a balance I was very happy with. It wasn't a quiet game of dominos at my local, but neither was it waking up naked chained to the Iranian ambassador on one side and Gail Porter on the other.

Six or seven of us went to Chiquito in Leicester Square for burritos, then on to the nearby casino to play roulette, and afterwards to Mahiki (not somewhere I would probably hang out on a regular basis) where we shared one of those 'Treasure Chests', which are supposedly quite legendary for Prince William ordering them. They're basically big wooden chests full of a not very strong cocktail with about twenty straws coming out (the only treasure involved is the profit margin of the proprietor). And we were all safely home in bed by about four in the morning.

For me, the thing that really put the brakes on was having children, but that didn't happen till a few years later, and I'd already slowed down a lot by then. Having a family was the first time what you might call an element of responsibility came into the equation. Even that wasn't so much a reflex as something I taught myself. Whenever I start to get a bit stressed these days, I think, 'You've got kids now, so you have to be responsible.'

〈 Magic was a big help with that 〉

But at the time I was starting work on my fourth album, I didn't yet have that safety net. If I was addicted to anything, it was work, and I threw myself into the early stages of that record with such abandon that I ended up doing little else but stare at a laptop for twenty hours a day. I don't know how Claire put up with it. If Mike McPhillips and CBT (which would be a pretty good name for a jazz-funk band) hadn't intervened, I think living with me would have become impossible.

I'd always convinced myself that work was the only thing that was really important, and if I could do nothing else but that, I'd be all right. Even during the first phase of the Mike McPhillips period, all I was thinking was 'I'm going to get better, and then I'm going to go back to work'. There were about three weeks when I didn't do anything at all, which was pretty unheard of for me. And in the months to come, there was a gradual process of me realizing that I had to do other stuff apart from make music.

Magic was a big help with that. By which I mean not the dark arts of sorcery, but the no-less-enchanted presence of my engineer of that name. Magic was his official dance-floor garage name, but now everyone calls him Madge — which is obviously not very nice, because it makes him sound like an old woman. (He would probably prefer to be called Mike, which is his name, but unfortunately for him it's mine too, and I was here first, so in the studio he'll always be Madge. But he's going to be Magic in the rest of this book, as a mark of respect.)

Magic is the only person I could be on a desert island with for any stretch of time without resorting to a bludgeon. He has an undimmed love for wine and UK garage, as well as a passing interest in microphones. His opinions and instincts cannot be influenced by mere money or hubris, but at the same time he never forces them on people, unless he has misjudged his dosage of tour-bus Merlot.

He first came along when I was making the third album, so he's worked with me on both sides of the CBT divide. But once I realized that division of labour had become essential to my continued survival, he completely changed my life by enabling me to have a bit of what other people have in the way of help. When you've got your own studio, as it gets bigger and bigger there's more and more stuff that needs maintaining, and keeping everything going becomes a fairly constant process. So you spend an awful lot of time in the studio just fiddling around and trying to make things work, and at that point some kind of delegation becomes essential, or you really will go completely nuts.

I've taken myself to the limits of stress a few times and just had to drop everything. But I've always been lucky enough to come out the other side in one piece. And when that happens, you're always especially grateful to the people who've stuck around to help you pick your life back up again.

17

Tim ideally wants to be managing Bruce Springsteen or The Beatles

While I'm showing a bit of appreciation, this is probably a good moment to say something nice about my manager. Tim Vigon, like me, is not a true Londoner. But unlike me, he's not interested in anything that isn't songs. He's really into Bruce Springsteen, and the first thing he did in the music industry was a Stone Roses fanzine — that's where his love of music started. So everything he's done since then, he's always tried to present it in a Stone Roses kind of way.

Given that pretty much everything I've ever done I've wanted to present in a Daft Punk kind of way, there's obviously been a certain amount of creative tension between us over the years. But that constant push and pull has always been a good thing.

The fact that all Tim's bands have such a secure financial position in this flakey coconut-shy of a music industry cannot be directly ascribed to either his father's Jewish blood or his mother being a Baptist. But in the same way that sociopaths have to learn to imitate a sense of sane non-violence from normal well-adjusted citizens, I have watched in wonder over the years at the incredible extent of his irrational loyalty towards lunatics like me and Rob

Harvey. This loyalty also extends to wasting his time supporting an intangible concept of togetherness through a randomly changing body of humanity and international finance like Manchester United. So perhaps I'm not the mad one after all.

Tim ideally wants to be managing Bruce Springsteen or The Beatles, but he still sticks with me, however far from that template I may venture. I'm sure part of him looks at the guy who manages The Red Hot Chili Peppers and Metallica and thinks, 'Why can't that be me?' But the fact that he's no more likely to achieve that goal than I am to be made an honorary member of the Wu-Tang Clan is our strength, not our weakness. When you have ideals in life, the extent to which you fail to measure up to them is every bit as endearing and valuable as any success you might have. If the Rolling Stones had been better at doing what they really wanted to do, which was sound like Muddy Waters, things probably wouldn't have worked out so well for them. By this I mean Vigon is amazing. I couldn't have done it without him.

It's not like the rock side of things is completely foreign to me. The late eighties, when I was growing up in the West Midlands, was the heyday of grebo, and I wasn't on some big campaign to define myself against that. When you're at junior school, I don't think you really define yourself at all — at least I didn't, except maybe by trying to copy what my older brother was doing. Once I got to senior school, grebo had kind of fed into grunge, and it

6 *We looked up what the next gig there was, and it was some band called Radiohead* 9

was all about Nirvana at that point. My friends who were into Mobb Deep went to another school, so there was definitely a period of time when I lived a bit of a double life as a part-time rocker.

The first proper gig I ever went to was Radiohead. We were in our early teens, and there was a kid I used to eat hotdogs with in the school canteen who had this plan for how we could radically improve our lives by undertaking a daring mission to the smaller of Wolverhampton's two main music venues. Not the Civic, the other one.

He made a convincing case. 'Fuck all these boring parties in people's houses where nothing ever happens,' he argued. 'Come to the Wulfrun Hall with me and we can get pissed, because you only have to get in and then you can get people to buy you cider.' I asked him what kind of cider he drank and he was, like, 'Strongbow.' He said it very emphatically, and I remember sitting in the canteen and thinking, 'I also want to drink Strongbow at this mystical place the Wulfrun Hall.'

We looked up what the next gig there was, and it was some band called Radiohead — whoever they were. So we thought, 'We'll have that.' Standing in the queue outside, we were all singing, 'Fuck you, I won't do what you tell me' — probably quite drunk already from the off-licence. Once we were inside, I remember us basically heckling throughout the performance (this wasn't as sacrilegious as it might sound to some people, as Radiohead were still in their corporate grunge wannabe phase; they hadn't discovered free jazz yet).

The 'You're so fucking special' song was quite cool though, because it had 'fuck' in it (there was definitely a common theme to the lyrics which struck a chord with me at that stage in my intellectual development). And my mate had surmised correctly re the laxness of the bar service policy. We were able to drink fairly unlimited quantities of Strongbow, so much in fact that he puked up in the cloakroom — always the hallmark of a magical night out at that age.

Looking back, this was my first proper experience of going out and paying money to see people make music. And I don't bear Thom Yorke any ill-will as a consequence of it. At the time I would probably rather have gone to see Snoop Doggy Dogg (as he was still known at that point) or some proto-backpacky thing like The Pharcyde, but for a timid fourteen-year-old like me, drinking Strongbow at the Wulfrun Hall with a load of grebos (or should it be greboes? You say potatoes, I say The Wonder Stuff) felt like a much safer option.

‘ It's all right, they were blanks ’

The funny thing about having now met people like P. Diddy and Jay-Z is the extent to which your illusions are shattered. When I was a kid, I used to genuinely think that the world of hip-hop was as violent as people made out. And even though obviously there is some genuinely nutty shit that rappers have actually done, as a general rule a lot of it is no more than window-dressing for the musical goods on offer.

Realizing that all rappers are entertainers was a gradual process for me. Obviously there are real gangsters out there too, and every now and then seriously connected characters do get involved in the music industry, but I'm not going to name names because I don't want Chris De Burgh coming after me. Or Mick Hucknall, come to that.

Grime, on the other hand, was probably even more violent than it was given (dis)credit for. And the reason for that was the relatively extreme youth of the people involved. When you're growing up in the inner city, or even in the suburbs, the time when you're most in danger of being physically attacked or even killed is probably in your mid- to late teens. If only because the guys in their twenties and thirties who are running things tend to get the younger ones to do their dirty work for them.

Most of the American rappers who get really big tend to be older, whereas people like Dizzee and Kano were in their mid-teens when they first came through; they're only in their mid-twenties now. Fifteen, sixteen and seventeen are the ages when teenage boys are at their maddest, and grime video shoots back in the day were really something. All sorts of scary shit went on.

As a general rule, meeting Jay-Z at a party at the Light Bar in Covent Garden is probably going to be a lot less dangerous than, say, getting a KFC in Harlesden. Although there are occasional exceptions to this rule. There was one time when I went to see Nas perform at the Brixton Academy, and a gun went off in the crowd. A fair amount of chaos ensued, but I had an access all areas pass I'd got off the promoter, so I ended up backstage. Nas, who's one of the wordsmiths I've most wanted to emulate over the years, was walking towards me down the corridor, and all I could think of to say to him was 'It's all right, they were blanks'. People do use real bullets sometimes in Britain, but happily not on that occasion.

There's no getting away from it, though. The only conversation I've ever had with Nas, and there it was: gun-talk.

❛ When anyone gets their first guitar, I think they always begin by doing the same things ❜

Some time in the early nineties, my brother suddenly got really into Jimi Hendrix. I don't know why, maybe it was the break-beats, but I remember thinking, 'This is a bit different', and starting to like it as well. I was into my own teens at this point, and so more able than I had been to make my own decisions about music. I was definitely into Led Zeppelin for a short period around the same time — the Beastie Boys had probably taken me there. But then Guns 'N' Roses' *Use Your Illusion* 1 & 2 came out, and we didn't need everyone else's Led Zep any more, because we had our own now.

Those albums were massive at my school, and one of my mates was quite obsessed with them; he was a bit mad actually, and busy getting into acid as well as drinking, which is quite advanced for your early teens. I liked the Dinosaur Jr record with the painting of the face on the cover as well, but the rock band who spoke to me most directly, probably because there was a little bit of hip-hop in what they did, were Rage Against The Machine.

They were really important to me, not just for giving me a suitably rebellious slogan to chant outside Radiohead gigs, but for the way their music sounded. It was constantly on heavy rotation in my bedroom, and when the moment came for me to start my first band, it was obvious what the template was going to be.

We'd got the loft-extension done by that time, and my brother was playing his drums in there all the time. Meanwhile I'd bought a blue Fender Squire out of *Dalton's Weekly*. When anyone gets their first guitar, I think they always begin by doing the same things — G/D/C, G/D/A minor. I can't speak for Jimi Hendrix or Jimmy Page, but I think pretty much everyone else gets started that way. If you heard the first songs I wrote on the guitar — and no one ever will — they'd be the same as any other indie kid's. At that age, songwriting is a kind of pastiche of all the things you've listened to up to that point — basically a low-tech version of sampling.

‘ We also got this bass player from a bit of paper on the wall in a record-shop ’

Pretty soon after I'd mastered my first chord progression, we formed a band. My brother played drums, I played guitar and added a bit of shouty stuff, and my friend Chris from round the corner did the rapping. We also got this bass player from a bit of paper on the wall in a record-shop. He was probably in his late thirties, and I was fourteen, so we had all the major demographics covered.

The band was called Harry and the Krishnas (I know what you're thinking: 'Great name, shame they never made it'), and we played Rage Against The Machine's 'Bullet In The Head' really badly. Even though we only ever rehearsed — we never actually played a gig — and probably only did that for a month or so in total, when I look back on it, this band is a very big thing in my head.

I was trying to be Tom Morello, who pushed me out of the way at Rock Am Ring in 2010 — or at least his security did. I couldn't really hold it against him: I was standing outside my dressing room at the time, and they were trying to get to the stage. Finally getting to see that band all those years later, you'd think they'd have been a disappointment, but they completely blew me away. I wish I'd been able to see them years before, but sadly they never made it to the Wulfrun Hall.

One of the reasons I really liked Tom Morello's playing was because of the way he'd turn his guitar on and off with a switch during a solo. Over the course of the long history of rock music, people have not done that nearly as often as they should've, in my opinion.

Once you're switching stuff on and off in the middle, you're basically crossing the divide between pop and electronics. And when Tom (I feel like we should be on first-name terms, now his security have pushed me out of the way) went for a solo at Rock Am Ring, I still didn't know how he was making the noise — he'd be hammering stuff high up on the frets with some weird pedal.

That was exactly what I wanted to do when I was fourteen. My ambition at that tender age was to take my guitar apart and put it back together so it would sound like no one had ever made a guitar sound before — and Tom Morello was still doing it almost twenty years later. I did manage to make my own wah-wah pedal at one point. Unfortunately, it sounded crap. I think you could definitely say I was looking at the instrument from a hip-hop perspective. And my guitar hero's playing technique was definitely informed by sampling (as well as completely insane jazz levels of practice), albeit in a far more satisfactory way than my rudimentary teenage songwriting was.

❛ I also love sweet potato, the vegetable that thinks it's a fruit ❜

When I look back at the music I loved when I was a kid — and my tastes probably haven't changed too much since, to be honest — the underlying theme seems to be a measure of extremity. I liked speed-garage because of the speed part, and in general I liked dark music — minor chords and harsh beats.

With the music I really didn't like, the common denominator was that it was quite girly. Not in the sense of having been made by women, rather in terms of not having an edge. Anything too singer-songwritery would be a good example, and I'm not really into pop either. I never have been. If it's a choice between the person who is pure pop or the one who used to be cool and then sold out, I'd always go for the latter, because there's more chance of them having a flashback and doing something interesting by mistake.

What else do I consider to be too girly? Well, not R&B for a start. I love R&B, even slow jams. Sometimes I'd even say especially the slow jams. They're really melodic, but there's something quite hard about them. And when you hang out with Jamaicans, they're just part of the deal.

I loved The Beatles, and I always thought Oasis were great, but I couldn't stand Blur. I always thought they went too far into the realm of campness and bitchery. Not that I'm totally immune to the appeal of those qualities in day-to-day life, I just don't like them in music.

The Blur vs Oasis rivalry was something I grew up with, but I always felt it was something the music papers made up for their own commercial ends. And the things the two sides were meant to stand for got really boiled down in the process. People who liked Oasis were meant to be meat-and-potatoes types who distrusted any form of innovation or anything pretending to be something it's not. A milkshake energy drink, for example, is a proposition your stereotypical Liam Gallagher fan would have theoretically run a mile from, yet in reality they'd be far more likely to drink one than someone who really admired Graham Coxon's guitar playing.

My marked preference for *(What's The Story) Morning Glory?* over *The Great Escape* has never translated into an obsessive need to maintain a strict separation between sweet and savoury. I don't mind raisins (or sultanas — whichever tiny dried fruit is available is fine with me) in couscous, for example. I also love sweet potato, the vegetable that thinks it's a fruit. I'm not a culinary bigot.

Someone told me once that the individual members of Blur

have all got sisters, but not brothers. I'm not sure if that's true, but I think it might be the gateway to a better understanding of the Blur/Oasis divide than the more traditional ones derived from social class or North African fruit-based cuisine.

‘ I feel like the first time I meet someone, I can always tell whether they have a brother or not ’

Even though I did have sisters, because they were so much older than me and weren't in the house when I was growing up, they felt more like aunts. My brother was the one who had the most influence on me, simply because I thought he was cool (feelings that were largely unreciprocated in my teenage years, although I did feel I'd earned my spurs a bit when *Original Pirate Material* came out). Obviously there can be an element of rivalry between males of slightly different ages, a fact to which Noel and Liam's turbulent relationship testifies, but Dan was quite tolerant of my determination to hang around with him as a kid, and I think that really helped to build my confidence, especially with our dad being so much older.

Two of my current best friends grew up with sisters but not brothers, so I'm not prejudiced against the brotherless as a social group. But I do think they have a subtly different approach to life, and I feel like the first time I meet someone, I can always tell whether they have a brother or not. And not just by asking them whether they prefer Blur or Oasis.

Looking back now, the extent to which Britpop impacted on the UK cultural landscape as a whole in the nineties almost seems like a throwback to the sixties, in the same way that much of the music was. I was excited about the way *A Grand Don't Come For Free*, and particularly 'Dry Your Eyes', managed to touch people across a similarly wide spectrum. But by the time my third album had come and gone, it was clear that making this big a splash, for me at least, was not going to be a regular occurrence.

Over the years that The Streets was operational there was obviously a massive shift in the way music reached people. With the decline (*The X Factor* excepted) of the old-school mass media relative to the more diffuse and fragmented mechanisms of the internet, YouTube and Twitter, it became much harder to buy your mum and dad a house with the proceeds of one single, but much easier to build and maintain a relationship with what Seth Godin would call your 'Tribe'.

Reaching out to the people who were really into what I was doing and expanding that connection into different areas is something we were really big on from the third album onwards. Ted has always been really up on all that stuff. And I've had my own reasons for being an early adopter, which I'll explain in the next chapter.

But probably the most important thing when you're committing a lot of energy to all those means of communication that were new and weird at the beginning of the last decade but felt like they'd been around for ever by the end of it is not to lose touch with the fundamental essence of what it is that you do. Tim Vigon was the king of that.

Whenever me and Ted were off in the Twitter realm, making our digital TV show *Beat Stevie*, or getting people to scan the barcodes off tins of Heinz beans on their iPhones to enable them to download a mix-tape, Tim was always there to say, 'Is this straightforward enough? The tour needs to sell.' In short, he brought the Bruce Springsteen. Everybody needs someone to do that. And while it would be a major distortion to say that bringing the Bruce Springsteen was what my fourth album was all about, the idea of making a whole album which didn't make any specific reference to modern life was certainly an attempt to see if creativity could still flourish in a world from which gimmicks and gadgetry had been temporarily excluded.

18

Product placement is just an extension of a visual metaphor

As obsessed as I've always been with music, in terms of the way I describe things and think about concepts, I'm actually a visual person more than a sound person. Different types of brain favour certain senses, and that's the type of brain mine is. The metaphors and similes I use very rarely relate to sound or taste. I never write lyrics that are 'sounds like . . .' or 'smells like . . .', it's always 'looks like . . .'.

When I used to have epileptic fits, I'd get this weird thing where I would see logos. Something happened in my brain and I would frantically be trying to work out what they stood for. You know that feeling when you see a logo on some clothes or some piece of electronic kit and you don't know what the company is; or even more generally, when you know you know the word for something but it won't come to you? It was a version of that frustration, but hyper-realized.

I would babble all this stuff to my dad about not being able to work out what a logo stood for. Someone once suggested to me that this was evidence of the extent to which I had internalized the materialistic mentality of hip-hop — there was product place-ment going on inside my own brain. But I suppose product placement is just an extension of a visual metaphor, so really what my brain was doing was processing its inability to work out the lexical cognition of the combination of that picture (the logo) with that concept (what the logo is supposed to mean).

As I got older, I started to feel that actually there were no logos, there was no company whose ethos and range of products these visual images were intended to encapsulate. My brain was just imagining them as a reflection of the fact that I was in a trance.

There's a guy in one of those really interesting books about how the brain processes sound — I can't remember if it's Oliver Sachs's *Musicophilia* or Daniel J. Levitin's *This Is Your Brain On Music* — who always heard the same piece of music before he had a fit, and didn't know if it was an actual piece of music or something he was hallucinating. This seems like the exact equivalent of my imaginary logos, only for someone whose brain has a leaning towards sound rather than vision. I can totally imagine the feeling of a sound and not knowing where that sound came from, so from my own experience I would deduce fairly confidently that the music he remembered didn't actually exist.

❛ I just kept pressing my nose against the screen and looking at the pixels ❜

That overwhelming feeling of misplaced familiarity is like a chronic version of déjà vu (by which I mean the mental state, not the garage club of that name in Stratford, which I never went to). But when you're experiencing these kinds of sensations for the first few times — when you still haven't worked out what they are yet — it can be quite terrifying.

My epilepsy started off as migraines and then it progressed to grand mal seizures. At first it was like looking directly at the sun till you get a speck in your vision, but that speck doesn't go because you've burnt a hole in your retina. Gradually that spot turns into these colourful things which get bigger and bigger. That part of the process probably takes about five minutes, and at the end of it I can't see anything but colours. Then I get this weird thing where my eyes kind of look off into the corner and they won't move. It's like I'm compelled to stare over there. I can't look away.

That was how my family would know what was going on. I was never in a position to tell them because I couldn't really string a sentence together — that's the point when you're about to go unconscious. Then I have the seizure, which lasts maybe twenty minutes to half an hour, then after that I'm out cold for about another hour. When I wake up, it feels like I've gone really hard in the gym or played rugby or American football or something else I would never normally do. My muscles are knackered, and I've got a banging headache.

When I was a kid we had a Spectrum computer I used to play on — the one with the really expensive joystick — and I used to do this thing where I would put my nose up against the screen, because for some reason that felt really nice. I don't know what that was about, but I presume it was putting me into the pre-liminary phase of a trance-like state. I just kept pressing my nose against the screen and looking at the pixels and I found that really relaxing. My dad would ask me what I was doing and I would explain very matter-of-factly 'putting my head against the screen', like it was the most normal thing in the world. It was, to me. But I remember doing it one day and having a migraine — which wasn't all that surprising as I was having those quite often at the time.

A short while after that I was in the front room of my cousins' house in Barnet watching *Charlie Chalk*, a TV show for really young kids that I liked for some reason. My mum was in the back room with my aunties. I don't think I had my head right up against the screen, but it was certainly quite close. And at that point I had another migraine, which my mum told me afterwards turned into my first fit.

Because my mum's always worked for the NHS, getting diagnosed was not a problem. That's where the NHS taboo in my family comes from, though my dad — God rest his soul — was a full-on NHS Nazi as well. It's a personal crusade really, not to bring down the NHS (which has always done very well by me, when I've needed it) but just to be able to talk about it in a balanced way.

❛ It's the cathode ray tube that is my enemy ❜

I presume a lot of people went to a lot of effort to reassure me that there was no stigma involved in being epileptic, because I never remember looking at my life in a before-I-got-it/after-I-got-it kind of way. But the one area of my existence which the epilepsy really did affect was TV and video-games. Because I was photo-sensitive, stuff flashing at a certain rate — either 50 or 120 cycles a second — would set me off. Unfortunately, TV goes at fifty.

On the upside, this meant I never had to do IT at school; staring at a computer screen for an hour was never going to fucking happen at that point. On the downside, it also meant not being allowed to watch much TV or play video-games, which was pretty much all my friends who weren't rappers wanted to do. My gaming days were at an end, at least until flat-screen TVs came in, because with them there's no flashing, it's just coloured pixels.

I have no memory of where
or when this is, but it looks
dangerous and I don't
condone it. That polo shirt got
a massive stain on it, which
is not in this photo, so it's a
bit like looking at a picture of
someone who died.

(© Rod Doyle)

Above left: This was very early one morning on an American tour. I remember we were on a long road with nothing around us for miles while they fixed this wheel. The sort of place you would never want to be unless you had a tour bus and tour manager.
(© Rod Doyle)

Above right: This is in Germany on a day off. I remember we had a good time in my room all day and staggered about some bars after. I've got some really weird video footage of me walking round that church in the background. (© Rod Doyle)

Below: This is my cousin Miles putting the words to 'Heaven for the Weather' on the window, ready for my family to sing. They named themselves The Barnet Pillamonic Choir and were all set to come onstage at Brixton, but I think someone bottled out.

Above: Just off the bus in Switzerland. This was around the time of the *Borrowed* album. It's always a surprise when you get off the bus as mostly, around Europe, you're in a car park, but this time it was a beautiful lake.
(© Rod Doyle)

Below: When there's a lot going on onstage it can be tempting to try to keep an eye on things, but you look really distracted. You have to focus on what's in front of you and forget the logistics. Which is why I didn't get the chance to see the massive orchestra behind me at the Proms gig. It looked great on telly, though.
(© Zak Hussein/ Press Association Images)

Top right: This really hurt. It pretty much ended my career in balcony jumping, which was long and eventful. I couldn't laugh for days. (© Rod Doyle)

Above: Filming the video for 'OMG' on one of the last big tours. I was pretty damn good at surfing at this point. I could read a crowd and know what I could get away with. The only really bad time was in Glasgow when I attempted a Moses and everyone fell over. (© Rod Doyle)

Left: This is what rock 'n' roll is all about. Forget the drugs and the parties. It's about doing things you've always dreamed of. Like drawing your face in a field next to Glastonbury. (© Yui Mok/ Press Association Images)

Above: Very last moment of relaxation during very last Streets show in Skegness. I was drinking like the old days and could probably have kept up with my old self. (© Rod Doyle)

Right: Apparently, I was right on trend with the *Miami Vice* look. I just liked *Miami Vice*, and part of the campaign for the *Hardest Way* album was to play with things a bit and with the ideas of what I thought success looked like. It was hard to manage bodily heat onstage with jackets. (© Miles Willis/ Getty Images)

Above left: On the steps of Marylebone Registry Office where every Beatle did the business, I'm told.
(© Ben Cannon)

Above right: Mum and Claire in France during our Continent-spanning wedding festival.
(© Abi Campbell)

Right: This is the dress. The most beautiful I have ever seen.
(© Abi Campbell)

Top: Claire and Amelia out and about. I can't begin to imagine how many raisins Amelia has eaten in her life.

Middle: Amelia telling me what to do. She's the first person to really do that in a style I respond to. I think it's because she always knows what she wants.

Bottom: George attempting one of his first unassisted sits. Every day something new. Very rock 'n' roll.

Looking back, I suppose you could use my dedication to making music as an example of the kind of creative things kids would do if they weren't allowed to waste all their time playing computer games. But I do think there's a big part of me that would've been driven to do what I did anyway. I can play games again now, but I still don't (well, except over Christmas, but we'll come to that later).

Obviously not being able to watch a lot of the TV shows everyone else watched must have had a psychological impact on me at some level, but it's not really for me to say what that was. It's the cathode ray tube that is my enemy, not TV itself. When flat-screens first came out, I was all over them before they'd even reached the shops. I know some people are frightened by technological innovation, but for me, the potential consequences of the absence of such progress are far more alarming. If no one had ever invented flat-screen TVs, I'd never have been able to enjoy *Breaking Bad*.

You don't see traditional TV sets so much any more, but Ted's got one and I can't look at it. The feeling I get if I do is a mixture of mild anxiety and this kind of mesmerizing element. It's almost like I'm a superhero — I can see beyond the image. Because the TV is flashing at fifty frames a second, it basically meshes with my brain.

The main reason I made my first album on a laptop was because the screens they had were the first ones I could look at for long periods. So I was an early adopter, but it was more for medical reasons.

I can feel a bit of a techie interlude coming on now, so people who are allergic to such things should skip the next section and start reading again at the words 'You can't listen to someone on Radio 1'.

The software I started making the first album on was Fruityloops, which had only just come out at the time. Nowadays a lot of dub-step people use it — almost in a keeping-it-old-school way — but the problem with it is, you can only really use it on a PC. I have got it on a Mac, because, technically at least, you can port it across, but doing that turns out to be an absolute nightmare.

‘ All the keys had melted and turned into these kinds of petals that were just floating in the air ’

I had to stop using Fruityloops when I got my first Mac, during the latter stages of *Original Pirate Material*. At that point I went over to Logic, and that's the program I'm still using now. If you're a musician you're probably more likely to use Logic, because that has a history of being a sequencer but is also a pro audio software. If you're more of an engineer than a musician, you're probably more likely to use Pro-tools. There's not much to choose between them, although the Pro-tools plug-ins sound better.

They're both made for the Mac. You used to be able to get Logic for a PC, but when Apple bought Logic, they brought the price of the software down to £200, which is dirt cheap, and then they just stopped making it for the PC, so basically you had to have a Mac to use it. Apple conspiracy theorists had a field day, but I thought it was really clever.

As far as I'm concerned, Apple can do what they like, so long as they make the best products. The minute something better comes along, I'll get that instead. There's no loyalty with computers. There can be a fair amount of trauma, though.

When I was recording my third album, I was heading over to

my friend's house with my laptop and a bottle of wine in my rucksack. You don't need to be a lifelong connoisseur of narrative twists to guess what happened next. I don't know how — I must have already opened the bottle at an earlier stage and recklessly pushed the cork back in — but by the time I arrived, the rucksack was half full of red wine, and the laptop with the only copy of my almost finished new album on it was completely submerged.

I took the computer out and hung it upside down, which is what you're supposed to do. But because it had the album on it and I was really impatient to find out if it had survived, I got a hairdryer out to speed the process along. This would probably have worked fine, except I was drying it while watching a film and slightly lost track of time. I looked up from the screen at one point to see that all the keys had melted and turned into these kinds of petals that were just floating in the air.

I ended up having to buy a new laptop and take it and the old one to this amazing repair-man in New York. He was working out of what was basically a tiny cupboard, and what he did was effectively reincarnate the soul of the old computer in the body of the new one. *The Matrix* was the first cinematic parallel which sprang to mind for the amazing service this man was offering, but actually he was more like the guy in *Tango And Cash*.

> ❛ You can't listen to someone on Radio 1 and take what they're saying as what they're really thinking ❜

This incident was definitely a potent reminder of the perils of the backpack. But hazards lurk everywhere when it comes to computers. I had to spend £275 getting my iPad repaired not so long ago, because my daughter Amelia had decided it would be a good idea to throw it across the room, just to find out what would happen. I'm all for youthful curiosity, but there are limits. At least, in an ideal world there would be.

Partly for the reasons outlined above, and partly just by instinct, I've never had any problem getting to grips with the fact that a flat-screen TV is better than a cathode ray tube, a smart-phone is better than one of those giant clunky mobiles from the 1980s, and an iPad 2 is better than an abacus. But I know some people develop an emotional attachment to a particular generation of technology and find it difficult to move on. Especially when they have a lot invested in the status quo.

I had a big chat about this over a coffee with Zane Lowe once. I love Zane because he is the biggest and most anal-retentive music fan I have ever met. He knows the name of the bass player in every band that never really made it. I know people say he boosts things up too much, but he does actually have an opinion as well. When I've done something he hasn't liked, he's told me, but it's not necessarily his job to give that view when he's on air. You can't listen to someone on Radio 1 and take what they're saying as what they're really thinking. Even Fearne Cotton can't genuinely think *everything*'s amazing.

Zane was struggling to get his head round the internet. And I think the problem he had was in not properly understanding the difference between active and passive attention. When you're on Radio 1 or MTV, you're getting a whole lot of passive attention. There might be millions of people watching or listening to you just because you're on, and you're never going to be quite sure of the extent to which they're really paying attention. Whereas if you transfer that to the internet, you might only be getting an audience of thousands, but that audience is much more valuable and enduring, because those people have actively sought you out.

Zane Lowe's approach to this is 'Where's the business?' But the problem with that attitude is that people have got a lot more choice now, so you can't necessarily rely on the clout of the old-school mass media to get your message across. Basically, you just have to do what you believe in and try to develop a small crowd of people who actually love (or at least really like) you, rather than a massive crowd that doesn't turn off when you come on. If you can get ten thousand people to spend a tenner a year coming to see you live or buying something you've released, that's enough to keep the business side of things going. And I think that's something we managed to do pretty well with The Streets.

> *⁶ On a Twitter feed, the uniqueness of each individual, which the festival setting conspires to conceal, is staring you right in the face ⁹*

I wasn't too far ahead of the curve when it came to blogging — everyone and the intern at the record company who pretends to be them was already doing it pretty soon after we were. But we got in on Twitter really early. When Twitter first started it was widely misunderstood as being just a one-way thing — the hungry masses gathering round to pick up the crumbs from the showbiz top table. It's true that some people have tried to use it that way, but they haven't tended to have much success.

The essence of Twitter is that it's a very public conversation. Your short message is automatically sent to all the people who have signed up to follow you, and then you (and they) can go to your feed and see absolutely everyone's responses lined up in a very long list. I couldn't hazard a guess as to what the average rate of reply is, but let's assume for the sake of argument that you'd expect fifty to a hundred replies for every ten thousand followers.

One of the things I found quite fascinating about this arrangement was how it simultaneously resembled and contrasted with the mechanisms I was already using to communicate with people. If I think about my first album, ultimately that was just a very personal thing — and for me, that was all it ever was — which hopefully, to the hundreds of thousands or even millions of people who heard it, felt like me talking to them one-to-one.

When I'm playing a festival, the crowd has more of a consciousness of itself as a collective organism as well as an assembly of disparate individuals. This can be an aspect of the experience that people really enjoy — being part of something that's bigger than themselves — but it can also be quite alienating, for the performer as well as the audience.

The cold-blooded financial rationale of a twenty-first-century rock festival, and I suppose of entertainment businesses as a whole, is to process the enthusiasm of large numbers of people into money as efficiently as possible. And when you're up on the stage, it can sometimes be quite hard to put that fact out of your mind.

The situation demands that you stop seeing people as individuals, because otherwise the sheer scope of all those different individualities will become overwhelming. So you dehumanize them, because you have to. And to see a sea of upraised arms waving as one on your command, like anemone in an ocean current, is not necessarily a particularly healthy way of looking at human beings. It certainly didn't improve Adolf Hitler's people skills.

No doubt there are some performers whose despotic tendencies are brought out by being in that position, although I've not seen as many diva outbursts backstage at festivals as you might expect. Johnny Borrell of Razorlight and Pharrell Williams of N.E.R.D throwing microphones across the stage is about as bad as it's ever got (it's always problems with monitors that get them — and I must admit, if you can't hear the music you're meant to be singing along with to an audience of a hundred thousand people, it's hard not to get a bit tense).

The dynamic which Twitter sets up with the people that are following you differs from the experience of playing at a festival in one key respect, and this is the thing which makes it potentially a bit more healthy as a means of interaction. On a Twitter feed, the uniqueness of each individual, which the festival setting conspires to conceal, is staring you right in the face. When you put something up there, you will get every opinion you can possibly think of in response — a 360-degree totality of different viewpoints. And unless you keep your feet firmly on the ground, scrolling rapidly from one to the next is liable to make you dizzy.

Of course when you're onstage performing to a very large crowd you know in the back of your mind that every person is different, but with Twitter the reality of that is much harder to escape. The people behind the opinions are revealed to you — or at least they are to me — in all their imposing uniqueness.

At a gig they're all together, en masse, but on Twitter they're in a long line, and you're having distinct interactions with every single one of them. Every few seconds you're seeing an individual, and then another, and then another. The analogy of the Queen shaking hands with the stars backstage at the Royal Variety Performance is not one whose implications I feel entirely at home with — for obvious reasons — but let's just say that look of bewilderment she tries so hard to hide is no longer a complete mystery to me.

Like any major breakthrough in communications technology, the full implications of Twitter are going to take us some time to process. Are we even meant to be able to instantly comprehend that many different individualities? When you're being passionately berated by American fans for your temerity in not doing any interviews — you thought you were saving them the trouble of listening to you prattling on about a load of bollocks, but it turns out you were actively shunning them — it does sometimes feel as if you're a guinea pig in some kind of not very well-controlled psychological experiment.

There are good ways and bad ways of dealing with the stress this causes. But the worst thing you can possibly do is start to look at it as a numbers game.

19

The donk of diminishing returns

If you follow the numbers on Twitter or the internet, all roads lead to Justin Bieber. Teen heart-throbs just trump everything. But when I look at my specific modest tally of hits — and it's very difficult not to — every now and again you'll get a spike and you'll think, 'How have we just had that?'

As a general rule, it's songs that people respond to. I find it quite reassuring that, unless you happen to be a skateboarding cat, you can't really compete with a new song by an artist. My music videos are massive compared to everything else we do. But our biggest ever individual spike came when we put a donk on Susan Boyle.

For those who are not educated in its ways, a donk is just a very reductive way of turning something into dance. Basically it's the simplest euro beat, where the music goes *donk, donk, donk*. It's terrible and rudimentary, but also classic. And it really gave Su-Bo a new dimension.

While we're defining technical dance music terms, I'd like to take this opportunity to revisit the issue of side-chaining. I wrote a blog a few years back about the *Tron:Legacy* soundtrack and how much I loved it, and gave it the title 'Side-chains and Wide Wailers'. I got stick off Ted for that because he said I was talking in riddles, but to me it's completely straightforward. Side-chains are the sucky-sucky sounds pioneered by Daft Punk's Thomas Bangalter which are now pretty much omnipresent in house music, and Wide Wailers are large-lunged vocalists in the soul idiom (Jocelyn Brown would be a good example).

The latter phenomenon is fairly self-explanatory, but the former takes a bit of technical background to get the hang of. A compressor is a dynamic controller, which means it turns the signal down when it gets loud, but up when it gets quieter, to narrow the dynamic range and make the whole thing sound fatter. When you hear a song played on the radio, it will generally have been compressed to within an inch of its life. And what side-chaining involves is putting a compressor on a loop to magnify the effect of the kick-drum.

Let's say you've got a loop which is going *dugga-dugga-dugga*. Normally, as that loop gets louder, the compressor would pull it down to make it feel fatter. But if you assign the control element of the compressor to the kick-drum, then instead of fattening up the sound of the loop, all it does is turn it down whenever the kick-drum fires, which makes the kick-drum feel louder, even though it actually isn't. That leaves you with that kind of see-sawing, panting-for-breath-after-running effect which will be very familiar to anyone who has ever listened to any record made by LMFAO (the theme song to MTV's *Jersey Shore* is the one that's hardest to avoid).

Maybe we should've side-chained Susan Boyle as well. Because if we'd paid too much attention to what the figures were telling us in the aftermath of our 'I Dreamed A Dream' donk triumph, we'd certainly have put donks on everything we did. Even though this would inevitably — and probably sooner rather than later — have left us faced us with the donk of diminishing returns.

The path I chose to take took me in exactly the opposite direction. What was the most appropriate creative response for me to make to a world in which rapidly evolving digital communications systems seemed to be changing the rules of engagement between music-makers and listeners on an almost daily basis? The way I opted to go was to try to come up with a whole album of musical parables which made no mention at all of any of the technological accoutrements of modern life.

I can see this looks like an obvious choice now, but at the time I can assure you it was quite a bolt from the blue.

❛ I do understand the appeal of the Spinal Tap *rock cliché arc* ❜

If I was to attempt to analyse my career in the guise of the terrifying neuro-linguistic programming guru-type character Tom Cruise presumably based on Anthony Robbins in the film *Magnolia* (and stranger things have happened), I would say that the ideals my first three albums were pursuing could be boiled down, in chronological order, to inspiration, structure and then truth. As far as my fourth album was concerned, people tended to think of it as a rehab thing. But that was bollocks. I was still doing all sorts, just at slightly less regular intervals, and the idea of sloughing off the detritus of modernity had nothing to do with giving up drink or drugs.

In retrospect, I can see why it appeared that way, but at the time I really resented the assumption that I'd gone on some kind of back-to-nature kick. I suppose that's because making an album can be part of the process by which you draw a line under a particular phase of your life. So by the time that record hits the shelves, you've already moved on, and the last thing you want to do is be endlessly reminded of the state of mind you've worked so hard to leave behind.

If there is a recovery album in my back catalogue, it's probably the third one. And a lot of what I was talking about on that record is stuff that was actually happening when I was finishing *A Grand Don't Come For Free*. However much people might want them to, the way your life unfolds and the way your work develops are never going to run exactly in time; there's always going to be an element of syncopation there.

Having said all that, I do understand the appeal of the *Spinal Tap* rock cliché arc. So even though I hadn't suddenly gone all philosophical in the aftermath of some rehab-prompted spiritual awakening, I just wanted to do something a bit different, and working within the constraints of not referencing modern life seemed a valid challenge for me to set myself (since referencing modern life was something I had become particularly known for) – like Slash making a record with no guitars on it, or 50 Cent doing an album with no gunshot sounds – I can totally understand why anyone who heard about what I'd been doing instantly jumped to that initial conclusion.

I would probably have jumped to it myself, if confronted with the same evidence. The *Spinal Tap* rock cliché arc is there for a reason – because there is a large element of truth in it. And that large element of truth is something no one in the music business can be arrogant enough to believe they're immune from. I don't think you can ever get away from it. If I'd done my fifth album fourth, people would've said, 'He's done a back-to-his-roots thing,' and that's another terrible cliché – re-embracing the blues riffs.

Because I'd gone to Prague to record an orchestra, and the album started with the sound of a Hammond organ being switched on, people maybe thought I was going to give it the full Jools Holland. But the fact is, my attitude to musical virtuosity never really changed over years.

❛ If I learn music, then I'll end up playing jazz, and I hate jazz ❜

When I was at school, I remember thinking, 'If I learn music, then I'll end up playing jazz, and I hate jazz.' I was quite insistent on this point as a kid. I didn't even like listening to music that wasn't the sort of music I was trying to make because I thought it might spoil everything. It seems quite narrow-minded, looking back, but I think you need that kind of focus when you're young, and in a way I was right. It would have caused me terrible problems if I'd suddenly got into jazz, whereas now I'm safely into my thirties I know it's still out there waiting for me. And if I was to give in to jazz temptation at this point in my life, the consequences would be much less serious.

That pervasive sense of not wanting to learn too much because you might lose the special thing you've got still endures. But on the other hand, Noel Gallagher can teach himself all the Ionian modes he wants and he'll still (I'm relieved to say) end up playing lad-rock, because that's just who he is.

I've picked up quite a bit of music theory over the years, without it changing either the kind of music I make, or the kind of music I'm into. So maybe a lot of knowledge isn't such a dangerous thing in this area after all. I've never actually learnt to read music, because I think it's an incredibly complicated way of saying something quite simple. Basically, music boils down to vibrations being divided up equally or not equally. When they're not equal, they're dissonant, and when they are equal, they're resonant.

The reason I love the piano so much is because it's such a beautiful way of seeing notes and understanding their relations to each other. If you look at the key of C, which is essentially all the white notes, and you turn each of the notes into triad chords, that gives you C, D minor, E minor, F major, G major, A minor, Diminished B, and C major again. If you create any sequence out of those chords in that scale of fifths, it will always sound right. And you can transpose the same relationship into any other key and that will still hold true.

The only danger is that it might sound a bit too sweet, in which case what you do is every now and again put in a chord that's just plain wrong, but you use that as a contrast to point up how harmonious everything else sounds. If you look at a lot of those really great Motown songs, that's how they're all done — really straight classical chord sequences, but with the occasional blue note thrown in to freshen everything up.

' Any kind of noodling is anathema to me '

I'm really into the Roman numeral chord system as well, which is just a very straightforward numbering scheme that they use in Nashville. Observant readers may have noticed the way I've paid tribute to it in this book's circle of fifths-inspired structural framework.

When it comes to music, I'm not a big fan of the smoke-and-mirrors side of things. I don't like any messing around when we're doing a session in the studio; any kind of noodling is anathema to me. If there is a keyboard player working with us, I'll basically say, 'Play something', then press record and — in an ideal world — that's it. If they're good, they'll come up with something nice. It's the same with the drums. And the guitar. Often as a producer your biggest contribution is not allowing musicians to talk themselves out of sticking with the first thing they did.

I am a complete control freak, but I want people to feel like I'm not actually doing anything.

Creativity by osmosis is the ultimate goal. In an ideal world, the music kind of makes itself, and you've not really intervened in any way other than to say, 'Stop noodling.' I'm not downplaying the significance of that contribution though — sometimes it takes a lot of effort to talk people out of using the knowledge they have. That's why Brian Eno will tell the whole band to swap over and play the wrong instrument — to mix things up a bit, so you can give experienced musicians the thrill of doing something for the first time.

It's all too easy for people to get to a point of professionalism where they're just going through the motions every time. At that point what you have to do is make a fundamental change to that process and then work really quickly, before their conscious minds have a chance to catch up.

> ❛ *We sent a demo to Bob Dylan first, but he was never going to get involved with the idea of being an old man* ❜

That was basically the trick I was trying to play on myself when I made *Everything Is Borrowed*. At that stage, I was still operating within the idealistic framework of trying to stretch myself in a new way with every record. Of all my albums, that fourth one was the hardest to make, because I gave myself such a very tight remit and stuck with it. And I still think some of the songs on it are incredibly successful, even though the man who reviewed it in Q didn't agree.

My favourite was probably 'Edge Of A Cliff', because even though it went through a really convoluted recording process, I was still very happy with the way it finally came out. The song had this kind of ancient guru character in it, who we spent a long time trying to get right.

We sent a demo to Bob Dylan first, but he was never going to get involved with the idea of being an old man. We also spoke to Cat Stevens, but he wouldn't have a bar of it either. After that, a guy who'd had a big Christmas hit on Warner's a few years earlier came into the studio and did some recording with Magic, but he just seemed really angry with the way he'd been cast aside by the music industry, which didn't give the song quite the serene feel it needed.

Then we did a version with Robert Wyatt, who was perfect. Me and Nick Worthington went up to the studio he uses in Skegness, and the vocal he did was great. I don't know why we didn't end up using it. I think it was probably owing to the fact that the lyrics kept changing and I didn't want to mess Robert around.

The way I work is a bit like putting a film together — everything's changing all the time. I've never encountered anyone else who does things the same way as me. Most people write an album and then record it over a few weeks or months in a big studio, but because I do everything myself I'll spend literally years getting from the first version to the one I'm finally happy with. And in this instance, we ended up going through five session singers to find the right one, even after the Wyatt version had gone by the board. It was very expensive.

Going to Prague to record with an orchestra wasn't cheap either, especially as, with the exception of 'The Escapist' and 'Heaven For The Weather', a lot of it didn't get used, much to the disappointment of my manager, who wants everything to be cost-effective (which I don't blame him for — it is his job).

> ‘ *Maybe philosophers are more like rappers than is generally supposed* ’

The idea of being on some kind of doomed quest for musical enlightenment was a big part of my fourth album, so it was appropriate that some of the most extravagant things we did never made the final cut. I suppose some of the restlessness of the whole process came from my awareness (certainly in the aftermath of the CBT interlude) that I was settling down a bit.

I sold my flat in Stockwell and had this fleeting idea to buy a place in Ibiza. That lasted for about three months, and I got pretty interested in a few places before I realized that we needed a place in London more urgently than somewhere to hang out on the White Island. At that point, Claire and I moved to the house in Highgate which we still live in now.

I've always had a very clear sense that I have to be able to sacrifice everything for music — that's something which goes to the core of me. If you think of someone like Mike Tyson (in his lethal prime, not in *The Hangover*), he came through a horrific childhood, and his unquenchable anger at the world fed into his total commitment to battering whoever was unlucky enough to be in the ring with him. That's not a career choice, it's an obsession. And even though I couldn't match Iron Mike for formative trauma, I always felt that when it came to music, I shared the same insatiable drive.

Once other considerations — your wife, or your kids, or even your own physical health — begin to assume equal or even greater importance to your primary creative motivation, you know the purity of that commitment is compromised. But in some ways, that doesn't have to be a bad thing. It's the people this never happens to who've really got something to worry about, a fact to which no end of broken showbiz marriages and ruined showbiz childhoods can testify.

The most explicitly philosophical and intellectually challenging thing that happened to me around the time of making *Everything Is Borrowed* was doing an interview with John Gray. If you want to find out what his work's all about, *Straw Dogs* is the book to read. *False Dawn* and *Black Mass* are good too, but *Straw Dogs* is the one where he maps out this kind of unanswerable void, a philosophical black hole into which all rival arguments disappear without trace. Because this book is so scarily dark, I thought he was going to be this big-talking guy. But when I met him, he was just like a history teacher. I was really impressed by that.

I did ask him whether he had kids or not, and he didn't. A lot of people who have kids do dark things, but maybe not so publicly — they feel the need to put more of a gloss on things. Your man Richard Dawkins is a really good example. He says all of this really dark shit upfront, but then at the end he tells you we will all be saved because we are such a great species. Essentially, it's Christianity wrapped up as atheism.

There are no happy endings in *Straw Dogs*. And I think if you had kids you wouldn't write a book like that. I know I'm not going to go to such dark places now I'm a dad. The death metal album won't happen after all, and even if it does, it will be more overtly the work of a persona.

Then again, maybe that's exactly how it is for John Gray. The same way Dr Dre doesn't really shoot people, because he's just a producer, but he says he shoots people and teenagers believe him (I know, because I did). Or 50 Cent put his name to that computer game where he goes to Libya to do a concert in Colonel Gaddafi's neck of the woods but it all goes a bit pear-shaped and he doesn't get paid so he ends up running around causing a revolution. (I'm not sure if that game is still on general release, as its already fairly tasteless premise has of course been overtaken by events to a painfully embarrassing extent.)

I haven't met enough of John Gray's colleagues to be absolutely confident about this theory, but maybe philosophers are more like rappers than is generally supposed. If their job is also to create a persona and use all the eloquence at their disposal to make as many people as possible believe in it, that would essentially make them MCs without jewellery.

20

Chris and Gwyneth were the exception that proved the rule

Robert Wyatt was far from the only example of me setting out to do tracks with other people but then the collaboration falling foul of one issue or another in the course of the particularly tortuous process by which my albums get made. That template was established as early as 'Dry Your Eyes'.

Chris Martin from Coldplay originally sang the chorus on that, but then the guy from EMI said he didn't think the song was a hit, and Chris didn't like the sound of his own voice on it, so that version got pulled. Even when I was in the papers quite a lot, I had very few brushes with what would be thought of as the world of celebrity on account of fearlessly keeping myself to myself, but Chris and Gwyneth were the exception that proved the rule.

When I first met them, I got the impression that Gwyneth was into my first album. I don't know why – I presume she saw her own lifestyle reflected in 'The Irony Of It All'. Either way, I went for dinner with my sister once in the vegetarian restaurant round the back of the Hammersmith Odeon, and we bumped into her and Chris, who were in there with Stella

McCartney and some other people, and went over to sit with them.

We met up a few times after that and talked about me and Chris maybe doing something together. I think my friend Rob's band The Music, who have the same manager as me, toured with Coldplay, so that was another connection. And when I wrote 'Dry Your Eyes', I thought the chorus would work well with him singing it, so I sent it to him. We met up in Primrose Hill at what was the band's favourite studios at the time (they've got their own now) and recorded the vocal, which I was really pleased with.

But once the song was done, the whole thing changed from being something that was between us, to something that was between our record labels. Negotiations got quite complicated very quickly, and in the end his people pulled it for reasons that had something to do with America. There were certainly no hard feelings from my side. It all worked out very nicely in the end anyway.

> ‘ *Deep down, what you really hate is not Chris Martin, it's yourself* ’

No doubt there are a few small-minded individuals out there who are relieved that my best-known song doesn't feature a cameo appearance by Chris Martin. I've always been puzzled by how furious some people — mainly music journalists, but not only them — seem to get about Chris's success. He's great live, he writes these amazingly unadorned but instantly memorable songs, and you can't say he's not a fantastic musician. So I'm with his good friends Kanye West and Jay-Z on this one.

A lot of the people who are most vehement in their disapproval seem to come from the same kind of upper-middle-class background as he does, and seeing him holding Glastonbury in the palm of his hand makes them feel a bit uneasy. But you can't tell them, 'Deep down, what you really hate is not Chris Martin, it's yourself,' because they might get upset.

There's something very British about being uncomfortable with naked ambition. We seem to have a big problem with that. But because I've spent so much of my life listening to rappers, naked ambition is . . . well, not quite my default setting, but it certainly bothers me much less than shit music does.

If we can take a moment to consider the example of The Killers. I don't think they have ever really been as good as they should've been. But if I was going to have anything against them, it would be that, not the fact that the singer says he wants them to be the biggest band in the world. No one ever gives Kanye or Jay-Z a hard time for being ambitious, so if you're willing to like that quality in them, you shouldn't hold it against Chris Martin (or Brandon Flowers for that matter) either. Jay-Z and Kanye certainly don't. And no doubt the fact that he's mates with two of the world's biggest rappers is the final straw for the Coldplay haters.

Kanye and Jay-Z definitely respect Chris on a professional level for the efficiency with which his music does the job. But it also helps that they come from such different places — not just geographically and socially, but musically — so they're not really in direct competition with him. Given the tussle they had over who got to release a song with him on it first (Jay won, Kanye was livid) you could even say that they like him as an expression of their competitiveness, rather than in spite of it.

No one's claiming these aren't two of the world's most competitive people (that's another league table they're determined to come out on top of). Kanye will slag off every other rapper in conversation. Of the big dogs in hip-hop, he's the one I've probably spoken to the most, and he's always been really nice to me. But he's got plenty to say about his more immediate rivals. Pretty much every other major name in hip-hop gets a scourging blast of 'he's not this' or 'he's not that'. It's hilarious.

> ❛ *I could probably play chess with Example or Wretch 32 and lose quite happily* ❜

American rappers aren't the only ones who compete like that. As everyone who has read the description in *Feel* — Chris Heath's Robbie Williams book — of the high-pressure game of chess between Robbie and Chris Martin at the MTV Awards will already be aware, our homegrown pop stars can be just as determined to put one over on each other. I love that book, and the fact that by chance I ended up reading it in the same luxurious establishment in which that incident took place, the Hotel Des Arts in Barcelona, only added to my enjoyment.

I have had a tendency to throw computer games across the living room in naked rage. But in general, if I'm playing a game I find it quite easy to allocate my ego to my music and sit down at the chess table with confidence that my sense of self is realized through my work rather than my performance on the board. I could probably play chess with Example or Wretch 32 and lose quite happily.

That doesn't make me a better person than Robbie or Chris, I'm probably just expressing my own competitive nature by exhibiting my capacity to rise above the chess-playing fray (therefore I win). It also doesn't mean I care about music more than they do. I think music is important to Chris Martin. Not so much Robbie perhaps, although I know some people speak very highly of his *Rudebox*.

I think the internet has changed this quite a lot – the success of Adele certainly suggests something's changed – but traditionally, making it in America meant going from state to state, doing every radio show, making sure your record label gave cocaine to all the right people and basically begging people to like you everywhere

‘ *They came up with a riff at their studio in Italy* ’

you went. When you're in America doing that, it is really apparent that you're flogging yourself every minute of the day. And there's something about marketing yourself in that way which is profoundly antithetical to the British character. It certainly is to mine.

That's why I wasn't too bothered when things went somewhat belly up for me over there after the second album. That's also why Oasis (and maybe even their one-time close friend Robbie Williams) never made it properly over there. And if you look at the bands that really do, they always seem to be the ones, like Coldplay or U2, who just don't have that shit filter. By which I don't mean that they're full of shit, more that they don't have that instinct to tell people to fuck off. Their attitude is more 'What do we need to do? We'll do it'.

I admire that approach, but have sadly never managed to adopt it myself. I've always had an incredible capacity for passionate self-destruction. And once my heart makes a decision that something is right, I'm incredibly bloody-minded about it, even if people at my record label tell me I'm sabotaging my own career.

That was certainly what happened when I did a track with Muse. They came up with a riff at their studio in Italy and sent it over so I could do my bit. Then some big rock guy mixed it and my A&R man started getting really excited. You suddenly get all these people at the label saying, 'This is gonna work on radio.' I've always been quite impervious to that kind of thing. When I listen to things or look at them aesthetically I just have an instinct, and once my shit detector has decided that something doesn't sound right or just generally isn't me, there's no going back on that decision, however angry my obduracy makes people.

I think once I decided not to go any further with it, Muse were going to put the song out as a B-side for a while, and in the end it turned up on the internet. In retrospect, there is a temptation to wonder what was the real reason for this collaboration never properly seeing the light of day. In the end I think it was just such a different creative process to the one I was used to, and because I wasn't in control of it, it was easier not to bother.

It would be possible (and possibly correct) to see that as ducking out of a challenge on my part. But the upside of it is that when it comes to those people who really do believe in The Streets, I can feel like I haven't let them down over the course of ten years.

It's good that people can clearly see where your decision-making comes in, and the extent to which it hasn't followed the same pattern as other weak-minded musicians who've made choices based on factors other than how the music makes them feel. People can see through that, and that's why even though they might be a bit reluctant to buy your last two albums, they'll still keep coming to see you at the Brixton Academy right to the end.

❛ Bands generally aren't that friendly with other bands ❜

Much has been said and written about the vital economic importance of the festival circuit to the twenty-first-century music industry, but very little about the social significance. I'm not talking about the crowds here so much as the performers, for whom festivals are the ultimate meeting place where any self-respecting rock or techno outfit does their musical socializing.

People tend to be quite conscious of their own little gang and what that represents. So bands generally aren't that friendly with other bands. First because they're quite competitive with each other, but also because reaching out in that way would be likely to exacerbate rivalries within their own necessarily tight-knit musical unit. If (for the sake of argument: I have no inside knowledge of an imminent personnel swap in this particular area) Chris Martin started talking to the drummer from Keane every time they met, then the drummer from Coldplay would have good cause to be anxious about his immediate employment prospects.

I never thought of it this way at the time, but looking back I suppose my particular situation was especially conducive to social interaction with people in rock bands. If only because I wasn't a threat to anyone.

‘ The Chemical Brothers see themselves as being very serious, so Basement Jaxx get on their nerves ’

The good thing for me was, the same applied in the grime world. People knew who I was, but whereas, say, Dizzee had to come to terms with a lot of very intense rivalries within the MC community, I've never been in a turf war. I guess the kind of stuff I do is so alien to people that what would be the point of anyone having a problem? Either way, I'm still friends with Kano, Dizzee and Wiley . . . although in the interests of full disclosure, I should probably add at this point that Lily Allen and I have not always seen eye-to-eye.

I have been quite shocked at the extent of some of the antipathies I've witnessed backstage, and the identities of those involved. For instance, Blur and Oasis had nothing on The Chemical Brothers and Basement Jaxx. I'm good friends with both parties so I find it hard to understand why they don't get on better, but I suppose The Chemical Brothers see themselves as being very serious, so Basement Jaxx get on their nerves by being a bit too frothy for their tastes. The latter duo are a mild-mannered pair who wouldn't say a bad word about anyone, but The Chemical Brothers don't seem to like Massive Attack much either, and no one could accuse 3D and Daddy G of being frothy.

Albums-oriented electronic dance acts seem to occupy their own quite stressful middle ground, somewhere between rappers and rockers. I think they generally started off with a lot of optimism and really being believers. But when it comes to touring I think most of them ultimately end up just pressing 'play' on a multi-track, because actually that's the safest thing to do. Stuff goes wrong, and you're travelling all the time. And all the way through dance music, that's what it's basically been anyway — pressing 'play'.

Orbital were the odd ones out in this regard. They were always just completely mad in terms of the sort of risks they were willing to take. And having a load of vintage analogue synths onstage is really risky, because you spend all your time repairing stuff. But they carried on doing it for decades on end, and I really admired that.

Because I was always more interested in going to house clubs than seeing bands live, that whole techno/rock crossover thing which happened in the early nineties slightly passed me by at the time (Daft Punk excepted). If someone asked me whether I thought Underworld's *Dubnobasswithmyheadman* was the best album of the dance generation, I couldn't really come up with a definitive answer. That would seem like the kind of question which is only relevant to people who prefer to consume dance music in album form, so it reminds them more of rock 'n' roll.

I did see Underworld play live in Miami once, and that was amazing, even though I didn't really know any of their songs. Except the 'Lager, Lager, Lager' one, and another with a weird arpeggio thing which someone plays on an MS20.

I was also good mates with Darren Emerson in Australia for a month or so a few years back.

I was doing the Big Day Out festival, so I decided to go out to Sydney four weeks early and live the Aussie dream, and for some reason I ended up hanging around with Darren a lot. He'd fallen out with the other two in Underworld by then – probably because he was much younger and came from more of a dance background – but I got on with him really well. We'd drink a load of white wine, then he'd start singing 'Fit But You Know It' and I'd be shouting 'Lager, Lager, Lager' back at him. By any objective criterion, we were a nightmare. But it was fun.

❛ Don't get me started on the Aphex Twin, though ❜

Don't get me started on the Aphex Twin, though. He's an absolute knob-jockey. I'm not generally one for speaking harshly of other musicians, but he's been quite vocal in his distaste for The Streets over the years, so fair's fair. I don't normally mind people not liking me, but people who don't like me who are absolute shit, I do have a problem with.

I spent the entire evening cussing him over the PA at a German festival called Melt once, after he came onstage with about twenty disabled people playing netball in wheelchairs. I realize that on paper this might look like quite an impressive spectacle, in a *Spinal Tap* kind of way, but to those who were actually there, it just felt really wrong.

> ❝ *Obviously Muse are officially a power-trio, so you don't see him on TV performances* ❞

Someone once asked me if I thought it was a coincidence that none of the people in bands I've become friends with have generally — with respectful apologies to The Music, Coldplay and Muse — been considered cool. That's a strange way of looking at things, but I suppose cool is not something I've ever either been (except for a few weeks in Williamsburg in 2002, and that was by accident) or tried to be. And the fact that there isn't a hipster bone in my body was always going to make it less likely that I'd become best mates with the guy from LCD Soundsystem.

Maybe there are some artists out there who have a checklist of cutting-edge peers they're determined to get to know. In fact, I know there are. But for me, the way you bond with people in the music business is the same as it is in any other walk of life: you just happen to come into contact with them and think they're funny.

For example, I got to know Muse after they head-hunted my ex-bass player Morgan to play keyboards for them. He used to be in a band called The Senseless Things, who Muse's bass player Chris was a big fan of, and rather than take offence at them luring him away, I thought it was really amusing that they liked the way he played bass, so they recruited him to play keyboards.

It was certainly a big ask for Morgan, because I think even he would have admitted that at that point he wasn't as good a keyboard player as he was a bassist. He's getting better now, though. Obviously Muse are officially a power-trio, so you don't see him on TV performances, but he's always there — one of rock's dirty little secrets.

They made it up to me by asking me to support them at the new Wembley Stadium, which was a really tough gig, but I think I did pretty well under the circumstances. The crowd were openly hateful. Their attitude was that they liked Muse but they didn't really like anything else, so it was highly stressful trying to win them over to the joys of geezer-garage. It just wasn't something they were comfortable with. I remember a girl standing right at the front with a banner that said 'Muse — Rock Music for Intelligent People', which says it all really.

She obviously had a very fixed idea of what she thought was intelligent and what she thought was really chavvy. But the one thing you learn from long hours spent hanging around backstage at festivals — and, I suppose, the message I hope people will take away from both the non-contemporaneous para-bollocks of my fourth album, and this chapter's extended survey of inter-band social interaction — is that those kinds of divides are like hands of cards at poker: they don't always fall the way you'd expect.

V

Resolution: *Computers And Blues*

21

If they stick with me till album number five, they know they can get a *Greatest Hits* out of it

There are three sides to every story. There's Bob Dylan's version, the rabbi's interpretation, and then there's the truth.

It's amazing how many of the fundamental issues of life come down to threes. From how many primary colours there are, to the tally of phone numbers in the humble drug-dealer's basher I swapped my iPhone for (my tour manager — the road wife — my actual wife, Ted, and that's it).

People have done economics tests where someone will have a stall selling jam, and if they have five flavours, they don't sell nearly as much as if there's three. Five is too much choice. Three is just the right amount. De La Soul weren't messing about when they sampled that song about it being the magic number. I'm not saying the sales figures of my five albums absolutely support this theory, but let's just say that if my record company had decided to set me free after number four, I couldn't really have blamed them.

As much as everyone tends to think the music business is all about the bottom line, the considerations they take into account in making that type of decision go way beyond mere bean-counting. OK, if they stick with me till album number five, they know they can get a *Greatest Hits* out of it. But also when the time comes to be signing other people, it will make them look good if they've stuck with me and my idiosyncratic personal vision right to the not so bitter end.

If you look at it from a musical point of view — which I doubt Warner's were doing, at least not in this way — the fifth is half the vibration of an octave. If you divide a guitar string in half, you get the octave. If you divide it again, you get the fifth. Further subdivisions in either direction would give you the third and the minor seventh. These are just the fractions of a vibration that inform a pleasing harmonic scale. But I'm not sure how harmonious the meeting would have been if I'd demanded a two-album extension on these somewhat theoretical grounds.

If I was going to write a self-help book, it would be subtitled 'What I can teach you about life from the perspective of the music industry'. Because pretty much all the knowledge I've ever acquired about people and business, and creativity as well, has been channelled through the music industry (both before and after I was a part of it). Some might see that as a pretty restrictive portal, but the evidence of my senses tells me otherwise. And there's a strange symmetry between the experiences of being on the outside looking in and on the inside looking out which I feel privileged to have experienced.

Wikipedia's capsule explanation of what symmetry is incorporates the very resonant phrase 'patterned self-similarity'. And I would now like to explore the meaning of that concept via the (seemingly unfeasible, but please bear with me) medium of my two encounters with Birmingham reggae legends Steel Pulse. One came when I was playing Glastonbury on the same day as them in 2008, the other more than ten years earlier, when I was sacked from a holiday job at their studios for dealing cocaine (a crime of which, I would like to emphasize – if only for the sake of my mum's peace of mind – I was entirely innocent).

‘ *Death metal bands tended to swallow them* ’

Let's be honest, the West Midlands does make the best reggae in England. It's up there with heavy metal, sarcasm and goalkeepers in any list of things Birmingham does well. And one important detail of my musical education I've so far left unmentioned was the summer between school and college (post-Harry and the Krishnas, but pre-Burger King) when I did work experience at Steel Pulse's studios, Rich Bitch.

It wasn't that kind of school-supervised work experience you get sent on when you're fourteen – I did that at Sainsbury's, and very depressing it was too – I'd sorted it out for myself. And even though I had a fairly realistic apprehension of the fact that this wasn't exactly the famously well-equipped Olympic Studios in Barnes, there was also a definite sense of it being a first step on the ladder in terms of ultimately finding work within the music industry.

Steel Pulse themselves were quite a distant presence. I only met them once, but the possibility of bumping into them again was quite inspiring. Most of the people I was actually dealing with on a day-to-day basis were of a very different musical persuasion.

My job was to repair SM58 microphones. Death metal bands tended to swallow them when they were trying to make that strange growling noise they think is singing. And when they weren't doing that, they'd be throwing them at the wall. That wasn't too much of a problem, though, as the microphones were simple enough to fix. All you had to do was take the screws off and re-solder them.

The microphone-abusers in question wouldn't have been Napalm Death or anyone you'd have heard of. Rich Bitch was the kind of studio where local pub bands recorded demos, although Sebastian Bach from Skid Row came in once, and Black Sabbath had their storage round the back, which was quite something.

When Sabbath came back off tour, that was the first time I'd ever seen a wardrobe in a flight-case. The idea that you'd have make-up and clothes in a box with wheels on seemed quite grandiose to me at the time. But the fact is, if you're on tour, everything has to be in a flight-case.

If J-Lo gets fifty flowers, a white sofa, a tree and some candles put in one, people don't understand why she's doing it. They think that's really terrible. But the fact is she's earning a hell of a lot of money, and the only disadvantage of her situation is that she never gets to be at home, so why not spend some of that money to make the experience of touring more homely? When you're not earning J-Lo's wages, it would feel like a bit of a waste, so there don't tend to be too many scented candles in my flight-case.

I didn't actively rifle through Black Sabbath's flight-cases. I just saw them out the back, thought they were amazing, and instantly ascended to the next level of insider knowledge above a normal person who might assume flight-cases only contain musical instruments. Such precious nuggets of data have the same invigorating effect on an ambitious teenager hoping to make his way in the music industry as those gold coins do on the Super Mario Brothers. And when you find out that Pantera and Sepultura travel with their own workout benches, so their roadies have to carry entire sets of weights in giant metal boxes — well, that's when a higher state of enlightenment really beckons.

Given that my ultimate ambition at this point in my life was to be Thomas Bangalter or the RZA, I knew there was still a little way to go. But fixing microphones was a start, and every little bit of experience I could rack up was probably going to be useful to me. With the possible exception of getting unfairly fired for being a wannabe drug-dealer.

I was a filter-feeder, like a prawn

It all started with a conversation I was having with the receptionist about drugs. Somehow that got turned into me selling drugs, and then all of a sudden the people who ran the place just didn't like me any more.

Historically, I'm a chatty guy, and receptionists are trained to talk. But the underlying theme of this rather painful memory is not that I'm attracted to receptionists, it's that at this point in my life I was definitely on the underside of the operation.

I was a filter-feeder, like a prawn passing plankton through its digestive system. If you want to be really healthy, you need to eat stuff out of the middle of the food chain. For example, white fish, such as cod — though maybe not so much cod, as there aren't many of them left. Tuna and other larger fish nearer the top of the chain tend to have a lot of toxins in, because they eat everything else, whereas those at the bottom aren't very nutritious, because they just eat crap.

There's definitely a music business analogy in here somewhere, but I can't quite draw it out.

The boss of the studio was a weird bloke with a moustache. He had loads of fish (in a tank, not to eat — well, at least not as far as I know) and a couple of rank German Shepherd dogs (I can still smell them now; in fact the memory is making me nauseous). You had this real sense that he must have been running the studio for at least forty years. He would've probably had a pony-tail in the eighties, but it was gone by the time I came into the Rich Bitch story — it was probably kept in a flight-case somewhere out the back. I don't know if the studio's investment in digital technology in the nineties was a good one or not, but there was a constant sense that money needed to be made by selling burgers at slightly inflated prices.

‘ *Everyone has a burger, don't they?* ’

It's very important to get the snacks right in a studio. Everyone has a burger, don't they? If you're in a band and you're rehearsing, you're going to at the very least have a can of Coke and a packet of crisps, and probably a Double-Decker. And if the guy running the studio is not delivering that to you at a healthy mark-up, he is making a huge tactical mistake.

It wasn't the moustached man who delivered the *coup de grâce*. There was a kind of studio manager with a curly mullet who looked like he could have been in Metallica. I remember him delivering the message that my employment was at an end. I took it quite well, even though I was definitely innocent. I was sixteen, which was old enough to understand that Steel Pulse could not afford to undermine their standing as respectable citizens by having an association with drugs of any kind.

In this case, as I said, the narcotic in question was cocaine, a drug of which I actually had little if any experience at that juncture. I don't want to incriminate anyone, but basically what had happened was a friend of mine had found some, and I was innocently mentioning that fact to the receptionist in a bid to seem sophisticated, and she (perhaps falling prey to a reciprocal impulse — a guy can dream) was intimating that her boyfriend might possibly be interested in such a discovery. That was pretty much as far as the conversation went, and in retrospect it's easy to see how someone overhearing us could have derived the mistaken impression that I was the new Pablo Escobar.

I wasn't happy to be sacked. It wasn't so much the pay, which was a fiver an hour tops, and I was under no illusions that what I was learning was bringing me any closer to my ultimate goal of going into a studio to record. All you're doing really when you're working at a rehearsal studios is plugging people in. By the time the band leave, not only will the microphone probably be broken, the drum-kit will certainly be in at least one more degree of disrepair than it was an hour ago. So as well as putting the SM58 back together, you're most likely going to end up re-skinning the snare drums (not retuning them, which is the interesting job, because drummers tend to want to do that themselves).

It was still a difficult moment to have to go home and tell my mum that this humble and not especially promising approach road into the music industry had suddenly turned into a cul-de-sac. Needless to say, I was quite discreet with her over the exact circumstances of my dismissal. In fact, most of this will be news to her, even now.

> ❝ *If that's not patterned self-similarity, then I don't know what is* ❞

An atmosphere of intense lethargy always seems to descend on me when I give up, or am sacked from, a job. My response to the Rich Bitch debacle was uncannily similar to the way I later felt when I gave up temping at Marks and Spencer's (around the time I was welcomed into the music industry by Damon Albarn), which in turn paralleled my mood when we switched off The Streets' Twitter account for the last time in 2011. As different as these three sets of circumstances might appear to be, there was definitely a common theme to the way I processed them emotionally.

The same applied to the long-delayed renewal of my short-lived acquaintance with Steel Pulse. They were on a couple of bands before me at Glastonbury in 2008 when I bumped into them again. My drummer Cassell had been watching their drummer — who is incredible, though Cassell's no slouch either — from the side of the stage. They didn't remember me in my teenage street hustler incarnation, but there was a really good vibe when we were all chatting together. What there wasn't, despite everything we'd all gone through in the intervening years, was any sense (to me at least) of us being different people to the ones we were the first time we met.

If that's not patterned self-similarity, then I don't know what is.

‘ My knowledge of reggae ’

My knowledge of reggae got better as I was doing The Streets. 'Let's Push Things Forward' had a ska element, but that came more from a folk memory of The Specials than me knowing anything much about the music that had originally inspired Coventry's finest. The lover's rock element in Kevin Mark Trail's vocals obviously came from him, not me. But by the time I was doing *A Grand Don't Come For Free*, I was obsessed with Jamaican dancehall.

There had been one obstacle to be overcome though, which was my prejudice against white people with dreads. I think the reason I've always been so hostile towards them, ultimately, is that what I perceive as unacceptable in their presentation of themselves is very close to insecurities I have about myself.

I guess this is just my version of the upper-middle-class music journalist's Pavlovian anti-Chris Martin reflex. I've pretty much spent my whole life listening to and making black music, and I've always been friends with rappers. And, no doubt like many a blues, soul or jazz fan before me, I've processed my sensitivity about this fact into a very critical approach to other white people who I perceive to be expressing their enthusiasm for black music in an inappropriate way.

It's quite a localized thing. They love reggae in France and Germany, for example, and I find nothing to object to in their enthusiasm, because they do it really well. If you go into a reggae club in Germany, everyone in there will be white, but they're so genuinely into the music that it really doesn't matter. They're not trust-fund revolutionaries swanning around UK halls of residence giving it the full Chris Blackwell. Those people really bring out my inner Paul Calf.

I was talking to Cassell about the nature of this antipathy once, when we were on tour, and in the course of the conversation I found myself saying 'I fucking hate reggae'. Cassell is not actually Jamaican; I think he's from St Lucia. But for obvious reasons I still had to spend the whole night explaining what I really meant. Which is that it's not reggae itself I can't abide — I've always been obsessed with various aspects of Jamaican culture, and by this time I knew what all the dances were and was really into Vybz Cartel — so much as a certain very English, very middle-class way of liking it. There's a lot of that in dub-step, I think.

❛ I always found it quite studenty ❜

Dub-step is very suburban, and always felt like a safe choice. I remember there being a real sense of a crossroads around the time Dizzee Rascal came out. The big new rhythms that established the template of grime were all really raw and aggressive. I recall my friend at Pure Groove saying he didn't understand what was happening. He used to sell records to DJs, and now he'd get ten teenage kids who would all come in together being really rowdy and buy one (according to his criteria) really badly produced instrumental between them.

At that point it was either MCs or nightclubs, and I always knew that my sympathies lay with the former camp. But if your instincts inclined in the other direction, and you were one of those people who basically wanted garage to continue, you were already on the road to dub-step by way of sub-low (both of which are essentially just slightly more experimental versions of garage).

It was the Magnetic Man guys from Big Apple records in Croydon who got it all going. Some of them were really young (I remember Benga playing at the club FWD when my first album was out, and he was only about thirteen at the time). And if people are into dancing at the kind of nightclubs you can go to without getting stabbed, you can't really blame them for coming up with sub-low and dub-step as an appropriate soundtrack for that environment. But it was never really my thing. I always found it quite studenty.

22

Then The Streets was going to come to an end

One thing I knew about the fifth Streets album was that it wasn't going to have a strong dub-step influence. The original idea was that the previous record, *Everything Is Borrowed*, was supposed to be about the past, *Computers And Blues* was going to be about the future, and then The Streets was going to come to an end. But it finished up being a bit more complex than that.

I definitely wasn't aiming for the extremes that I'd played out with the previous records. The first album was extremely British, and quite odd; the second album was extremely a story; the third album was extremely extreme; the fourth album was extremely philosophical; whereas the last album was always going to be extremely *balanced*.

The plan was to combine elements of all its predecessors, and hopefully bring them together in a satisfying way, but it was always going to be the most formulaic record I'd ever made. I knew the kind of songs I was going to write — each one would involve outlining a genuine human drama of some description, and then trying to sum it up with the chorus in a way that wasn't straightforward — and I was determined to stick to that template. It was hard to see what other direction I could go in. Had I started experimenting again at that point, it almost certainly wouldn't have worked, and the only other way to go was backwards.

' *There's no margin in being the Liberace of geezer-garage* '

If I hadn't already known *Computers And Blues* was going to be the last Streets album when I started work on it (which I did), I certainly would have by the end. I never said I was going to retire, just that I wouldn't be doing this particular thing any more. And why would I? People have always liked the idea that there's something honest about The Streets — and it has been honest. But it couldn't stay that way if I allowed it to become a parody of itself. There's no margin in being the Liberace of geezer-garage.

It took me a bit longer than I'd expected to hang up those sequinned Patrick Cox platforms. By the summer of 2009, the bulk of the fifth album was done, and it had been going OK, but I suddenly seemed to be ill all the time. I thought it was tonsillitis, and I almost had my tonsils removed; the surgeon said, 'I'll do it for you, but I'm not sure that's what it is.' Then I did an American tour on which I seemed to get really ill pretty much every other day, to the extent that I had to spend alternate days in bed, and without the justification of chemical or alcoholic over-indulgence I would once have been able to claim.

The gigs were great, but some of them were a bit weird. One night I got really angry with my ear-piece and ended up smashing it on the stage. By the time I got on the plane back to England I was running a massive fever, and shortly after returning home I was diagnosed with ME. They said I'd probably had it for the previous six months, although presumably the time when I was unable to sleep in Notting Hill and ended up going for the cognitive behaviour therapy might have been a bit of an early warning.

' The ME is not something I want to say too much about '

The groundwork I'd done then in accepting that it might be necessary for me to do something else with my life other than stare at a laptop for eighteen hours a day certainly stood me in good stead at this point. I was in hospital for a while, but basically the only way to treat it was to turn everything off and stop doing anything that might be even vaguely associated with work.

ME is a condition which is quite widely misunderstood. Some lives are absolutely destroyed by it. It's not just the embarrassment of having this thing that lots of people don't really believe exists. I also think in my case people find it very hard to believe that you could (as I did) drive yourself into such a state simply by spending too long writing music. I'd probably struggle with that explanation too, if it hadn't happened to me.

Beyond that, the ME is not something I want to say too much about. It's not that I'm frightened of getting hate mail, just that it wasn't really that big a deal, and I'm incredibly lucky to work in a field where I can effectively take a year off to get better without doing myself any lasting professional damage. If you take a big chunk of gardening leave in the music industry, people generally just assume you're in rehab for a coke habit and leave it at that.

What I was actually doing was watching films and going to art galleries and leading a really contemplative life. You've got to keep doing stuff, but not too much, and finding that sweet-spot is the road to recovery. As time went on, I found I could get a bit done in the morning. My daughter Amelia would wake me up around 6.30. I'd usually be in bed by ten in the evening, and I'd need a bit of a rest in the afternoon – not actually going to bed, just thinking about stuff that wasn't work. But there are still plenty of hours left in the day on that kind of schedule if you use them carefully.

Once the summer of 2010 had arrived I was feeling well enough to do a few more songs. One of them was the single 'Going Through Hell', the other was 'Trying To Kill ME'. I shouldn't really have been working at that point – which is kind of what the second of those songs was about – but I was on my own path. I knew what I needed to do, and feeling you're regaining control of your capacity to push your luck a bit is a big part of making a full recovery. So I wrote the song about having to stop working overnight and recorded it in a day, then had a bit of a relapse.

❛ Mum was like, 'Actually, that bit is true' ❜

Giving up work, whether on a short-term or a long-term basis, is not something people in my family traditionally do easily. I'm very like my dad, and he found it quite hard to come to terms with the idea of himself as a retired person. I'm not sure what he'd have liked me to say about this, but I think maybe he defined himself by his work a little more than he realized. So when he found himself being round the house a bit more with time on his hands, he gradually felt like he didn't have a role, and just gave up a bit.

Seeing that happening certainly shaped my determination never to stop working. And I think it's even harder if you've got a normal job, because then you're probably doing either fifty hours a week or nothing. My dad had always been self-employed – he was an entrepreneur, as much as anything – so if ever there was a time when work slackened off a bit, he would always have turned that into a new business opportunity. And I think it was knowing he wasn't going to be able to do that any more that was so difficult for him.

You might say what he went through towards the end of his life sounds like depression, and in a way it was. But I wouldn't describe either of us as depressives. We're more bipolar, which sounds the same, but it's not.

At his worst, quite near the end, my dad was briefly sectioned under the Mental Health Act. Mum went in for a visit and they called her aside and said, 'We just need to talk to you about some of the things your husband's been saying. He told us today that his son has been on *Top Of The Pops* and is a pop star.' So Mum was like, 'Actually, that bit is true.' Dad was always up and down to a degree, but in general he led a very stable life, and it was only towards the end that being slightly bipolar became a challenge to him. The whisky from nine a.m. probably hadn't helped.

> ❛ *The essence of being an adult is trying to conceal that* ❜

In the course of the ME (or chronic fatigue syndrome, or Eustachian tube dysfunction, or whatever it was that went wrong in my head), I read a lot of books. Partly in the aftermath of that, and partly just from being on the earth for thirty-three years, I feel like I've now got quite a clear perspective on the ways in which I'm different to pretty much everyone else in my life. The main clear blue water I can detect is in terms of the intensity of the divergent emotions I will feel throughout the average day.

Obviously everyone's moods fluctuate a certain amount, but waking up really happy and then an hour later being in a terribly sad place is pretty much the norm for me. I find that the essence of being an adult is trying to conceal that. But anyone who knows me will be familiar with the ridiculous range of emotions I'll experience throughout the average day. It's mainly down to what I'm working on — either what's wrong with what I'm doing, or what's right with it.

My dad was very similar. I've never been sure if I've been saddled with more of that up-and-down tendency than he was. It may be that I have it slightly worse, or it may just be that the nature of my working life has tended to exacerbate the rhythm of it, at the same time as giving me more opportunity to dance (figuratively speaking: I was never much of a body-popper) to that particular beat.

People who are bipolar will just go out and buy a motorbike for no reason. Dad used to do that kind of thing sometimes; he'd just come back from work and show us the new car he'd bought, or tell us about some unexpected activity he'd planned for the next day. Finding out why he'd done this certainly explained a few things.

Sometimes the spontaneity of approaching life in that way can be very exciting. But it can get you in trouble as well. They call it mania, don't they? When you're up, you take incredible risks and completely disregard your environment. And then when you're down, well, you're down.

‘ It's probably only a mad person who can feel all the emotions of an hour's worth of pop music ’

I'm the same, but for me that risk-taking behaviour generally manifests itself (spread-betting excepted) in making music that is very uncompromising. When that's what's happening, I generally feel like I'm doing exactly what I need to be doing. And when it's not, my sense of displacement and irritation can become quite overwhelming.

One time when I really notice those successive waves of different feelings is when I'm onstage. It's probably only a mad person who can feel all the emotions of an hour's worth of pop music; sometimes I wonder if you can even sing one song properly without being slightly bipolar. That's why if you're performing for a living it helps to be a bit of a diva. People like Barbra Streisand and Mariah Carey can convey everything they need to and it comes quite naturally to them — you can see them just riding the wave.

I go the opposite way. Rather than refusing to go onstage unless someone gives me a puppy, I tend to make people around me quite frustrated by being too matter of fact about everything. But the truth is, I need to be that way if I'm going to get through the experience in one piece. Someone might tell me that 'Dry Your Eyes' is the perfect summation of how they felt at a particular moment in their life, and on one level I understand and appreciate that — I must do, otherwise I could never have written the song in the first place — but at the same time, when I'm performing it live, it's probable that the only thing I'll be thinking about is what I'm going to say at the end of it.

I've not actually listened to that song in years. I've sung it a lot, and I've been channelling the very core of the emotion in the lyric as I've done so, but at the same time all I was thinking about at the time was getting the words right, and how best to get from the end of it into the next one. My mind was elsewhere, because it had to be.

It wouldn't be possible to experience the emotions of the song anew every time you performed it. At least, not for me. Maybe the people who can't stop themselves doing, or even trying to do, that are the ones who wind up dead at twenty-seven.

⁶ Some people end up cuddling the song, and the song ends up being shit ⁹

Maybe it sounds heartless to describe it as more of a functional thing. And if you say that a performance can't be a complete experience of the song, but you can enjoy the function of executing that song successfully, it probably makes you sound more like a golfer or a motor-racing driver than an actual human being. But it's not a question of being a cold or unemotional person, it's a question of how your emotions are arranged.

It's a bit like having a child. You love the child more than anything, but you have to bypass some of your feelings in order to be a good parent. For instance, one of the things I want to do is constantly cuddle my daughter Amelia. But for me to grab hold of her and do that would actually be really annoying for her; she wouldn't like it at all. So I have to pick my moments through the day.

Conversely, when she's being an absolute mentalist — say we're in a restaurant and all she wants to do is not eat anything and lie on the floor screaming — you don't want her to be like that but you have to keep your response within the realm of what is actually going to help the situation. Take control of your emotions and channel them in a pragmatic, manageable way. Essentially what you're doing is using the power of your love to help you take responsibility.

That's how it is with a song. It's an emotional thing, and I'm an emotional person, but if that relationship is going to operate successfully, I can't just be cuddling the song. Some people end up cuddling the song, and the song ends up being shit. It ends up like one of those kids in a sitcom who are too old to be living with their parents and don't have any life of their own. Or one of those rappers who do great things but then drive you mad by going on about their daughter in public the whole time. (Yes, Eminem, I'm talking to you. Please shut up about Haillie, for her sake as well as ours.)

❝ It was a bit like the Windows operating system ❞

All that long year when I essentially just had my feet up, Magic was hard at work. My studio had become incredibly hot to work in. It was a bit like the Windows operating system — it had been around for such a long time and had so much other stuff bolted on to it that it had ended up as a bit of a mess. So he packed all the gear away, and we ended up with a big empty space.

We set up one half of it as the control room, and acoustically rendered the other using a recipe from the internet, as implemented by the proverbial Polish carpenters. The end result was, and is, amazing. It's as good as if not better than a lot of the really big places in LA. You can record anything in there and you don't get reverb.

Magic and I have got a really efficient set-up developed too. I can come up with a lot of ideas really quickly, but I'm also very, very impatient, and I tend to get tired by lunchtime. So I usually work for about six hours and then go off and do something else while whatever needs to get sorted out gets sorted out. I need to be very regimented, but so long as I don't do more than what feels like a half-day to me, and I spend the rest of the time just kind of thinking about it but not really doing anything, then I don't go mental. Whereas if I work straight through from six in the morning till eight at night, I start having weird dreams, and the next thing I know I'm on the edge of getting swept away.

23

I hope I'm not going to sound like Alanis Morissette if I describe this as ironic

Whatever it was about The Streets that had become a burden, touring was always easy. The creativity — writing the albums — was the hard bit. But singing a load of songs you've already written (in some cases ten years earlier) is not exactly taxing, is it?

When I first got asked to do live shows, I regarded them as a ridiculous imposition, and fundamentally my position on that never really changed. The funny thing is — and I hope I'm not going to sound like Alanis Morissette if I describe this as ironic — that by the latter stages of The Streets, this aspect of the job which I had regarded as a total irrelevance had become central to the economics of the whole operation. Everything else was funded by the festivals.

Maybe this makes me a hypocrite, but in the end I'd come round to the idea that even though touring was easy and not inherently creative or really of any great value, the value was in the songs, and as long as I'd got the songs right, the tours would continue to sell, and I could rely on them to keep the whole thing going. It's not quite like banking your winnings on *The Weakest Link*, but it nearly is.

The idea of just turning up and singing the songs might seem a bit cynical, but when I think about the people I was really into when I was a teenager, like Daft Punk and Rage Against The Machine, I just wanted to see them perform their music in a way that was recognizable to me. It wouldn't have bothered me when I was a teenager that both those bands do pretty much the same show every night, and it doesn't bother me now. It's still a great pleasure for me to look at them while they repeat themselves. Because it's not enough to just listen to it on your iPod. You want to be in the same room as the person — it's like a book-signing.

> ‘ *I've always had the feeling that no one can really hear you and they wouldn't be interested anyway* ’

Because I'm an idealist in a slightly different way to Tom Morello — and I've not done as much jazz practice — I always tried as hard as I could to make every show about that particular moment. We had to have this balance of a set sequence of songs that were rehearsed within an inch of their lives so we'd know the timings inside out, and then we could afford to play around a bit within that. Basically the gaps between the songs end up being the fun bit.

I never thought there was too much to live up to in terms of the tradition of live hip-hop. Obviously rap started out as a live thing in New York in the early days, but as soon as overseas tours started to happen, it was mostly just a question of getting paid and then going home to make amazing records in the studio.

Outside of local open mic shows, I don't remember seeing any famous rapper perform live when I was growing up, except Bustah Rhymes at Aston Villa leisure centre. I've never really been into rap shows subsequently. In fact, I'm trying to think of any I've really enjoyed.

I think The Roots are great as a live band, but that's more of a festival thing. And The Fugees were really more of a rock band with a very good singer. I do remember seeing Ghostface from the Wu-Tang be really good in Chicago once. That was one of the few times I've had a sense in a live performance of someone being a wordsmith, and the way this might relate to the delivery of their lyrics in that context.

I don't really think about the words when I'm onstage — I've always had the feeling that no one can really hear you and they wouldn't be interested anyway. Certain rappers — Eminem; Professor Green in his Beats incarnation was another one — are really good off the top of their heads, but most aren't like that. And even the ones like those two who've come up through a lot of MC battles will generally just say what they've written. Obviously you've got to be quick on your feet once you're onstage, but that doesn't mean you won't have written it down first.

A lot of the problems with live hip-hop come from the venues. No one can do it like a really good MC at a rave, but the static nature of an arena or stadium performance does the music no favours. Dance music is the same, once you get to a certain level. It's just a bit odd seeing a guy DJing onstage at the Brixton Academy — it doesn't quite fit — whereas rock music was (and is) designed to tour those sorts of venues. If you see someone like Muse at Earls Court or Wembley Arena, it's obvious that the music has been designed and developed to fill spaces of that nature.

My strategy for overcoming the problems traditionally presented by trying to perform hip-hop in larger live arenas remained fairly consistent throughout a decade of The Streets: it was basically to scream and shout a lot. Beck was a big influence. I remember watching him do a performance at Glastonbury once. It was Saturday afternoon in the mid-/late nineties and it was pissing down (I could see that clearly, even watching at home on the telly).

❛ I ended up getting really spotty because I was using hand-wipes to wash ❜

I'd never been to a festival before I started performing at them, and since then I've been to Glastonbury once as a punter. It rained for the whole three days, and I ended up getting really spotty because I was using hand-wipes to wash. I certainly wouldn't describe it as a high point. I've had much better nights there when there's been a tour-bus to take me home.

Such luxuries were still a few years in front of me when I was watching Beck. The impression I gleaned from watching his performance was that he had sized up what was potentially a very depressing situation, and decided simply to scream and keep on screaming until the crowd thought he was so mad that they might as well go with it. The lesson I took from this, and filed away for later use, was that if you're unbelievably committed to having a good time onstage, if you just try and knock people off their feet with pure shouting, they do actually end up joining in.

❛ I probably have a very narrow-minded idea of what people having a good time is ❜

You have to remember that every single person who goes to a concert, however jaded they are, and however much they're from

London, wants to have a good time. But sometimes you have to remind them of that fact — which can take a bit of doing, and there's nothing really cool about this process. In fact, it often involves being about as uncool as you can possibly get.

As far as I'm concerned, the whole playing live experience basically comes down to wanting to be sure I've earned the money. It's the same professional pride-based approach that I had from the beginning with the music. It was always very important to me that my songs should serve some kind of straightforward purpose, and the same applied to my live shows. My first concern was that they should live up to the Platonic ideal of what a live performance should be, i.e. people should have a good time.

I probably have a very narrow-minded idea of what people having a good time is. But I did always notice a big change in every crowd after we did a 'Go Low' (where I'd make everyone crouch down on their haunches) or a 'Go Moses' (when I'd stage a budget reconstruction of the parting of the Red Sea using human waves).

We all feel a need to be consistent with our statements and our actions. If everyone's standing there doing nothing while you perform, it's probably because they had an idea in their heads at the beginning of the show which they are trying to be consistent with, and that idea was 'I didn't come here to dance; I've paid my money and I'm going to see if they're any good before I respond in any physical way'.

At that point, your job as an entertainer is all about changing the fundamental premise your audience is striving to be consistent with. And the simplest and best way to do that is to point out that deep down, they do want to enjoy themselves. There's definitely some neuro-linguistic programming in there —

basically, a lot of what I do is Anthony Robbins. But I'm trying to encourage people to let go of their inhibitions for their own good, rather than as part of the slightly seedy seduction strategies NLP is usually used for.

‘ *Obviously this is not how The Grateful Dead did it* ’

You want as many people as possible to be dancing, because then suddenly there's this 'Everyone's having a really good time' meme, which everyone will want to be consistent with. If people do participate, then they feel like they've put something into the show themselves, and at that point they're more likely to get something out of it. I know this sounds a bit like something a drama teacher might tell you in the vain hope of drumming up enthusiasm among the cast of the school play, but in my experience it is actually true.

I also realize that other strategies for live performance are available. Obviously this is not how The Grateful Dead did it, and they've done amazingly well. And I've been knocked off my feet over the years by plenty of bands — Pink Floyd would be a good example — whose approach is the complete opposite of everything I try and do. There's no talking between songs. There's hardly even any singing really. Looked at through my value system, everything goes on too long and there's nothing really happening.

It's like a Sofia Coppola film. Every scene is over-extended, but somehow the whole thing seems to work. That one about the rock star in the hotel has got some really, really long scenes in it, where he's just sitting there watching the telly for about a minute and a half, and you're watching it thinking, 'When are you going to say cut?'

❛ Knowing when to stop is a very important skill ❜

Knowing when to stop is a very important skill. In the run-up to *Computers And Blues* coming out, we had this timer counting down on the website. A couple of weeks before the release date I was getting really stressed out, thinking, 'What am I going to do when it counts down to nothing?' So I thought, 'Fuck it. When the album comes out, I'm just going to switch it off.'

The people at 679 weren't too happy about this. Closing down your website on the day your new album hits the streets is not a conventional promotional mechanism. In fact, it's thought to be just about the worst thing you can possibly do. And I'm sure it probably did contribute to the lack of label backing and Radio 1 support for the record. But not in a bad way. I don't suppose there'd have been too much of either of those things flying around anyway — I wasn't expecting it to be a priority release for anyone, other than me — and at least by shutting everything down we took control of the situation.

As if to reward us for taking our destiny into our own hands, the tour which followed was amazing. All the dates sold out, and the summer festivals after that were some of the best shows I've ever done.

Let me tell you something about melodrama. Melodrama is not overacting, it's under-motivation — stuff happens without enough reason. The last Streets shows were that in reverse. We never mentioned the fact that it was a farewell tour, because we wanted any emotion that was there to be induced by the actual situation rather than expectations we had deliberately raised.

Because the finality of it all went largely unspoken, that made it all the more powerful. All the reviews interpreted these performances as being really emotional, and they did have an emotional impact, but that impact was heightened by me only ever alluding to the fact that something was ending once, right at the end. At that point I'd thank everyone for their support over the past ten years, and I'd get this great big roar of stuff back, which felt really special.

Essentially it was the opposite of *The X Factor*, when they show you those endless close-ups of young men and women and their friends and families in floods of tears because they haven't got to go to Judges' Houses, but the overall effect is to diminish your capacity to have sympathy with them, not to enhance it. Even when I was showing my arse to bring The Streets' live odyssey full (ahem) circle at the 2011 Reading Festival, I was still a poster-boy for emotional continence.

❛ It's the screening in the cinema that you get your money from ❜

Aesthetically, as a tactic, bringing the curtain down with a bit of a flourish seems to have worked. The album didn't sell, but it never really felt like that was the objective (at least, not to me). The objective was to take something which was potentially going to look like it was winding down and say, 'This is the end' in a very deliberate way to make an event out of it. People don't often do that. They generally make things go on for much too long.

It wasn't about closing with fireworks. I didn't have that much regard for myself to think that was how it was going to feel. I guess I was at a point after *Everything Is Borrowed* where I'd become so un-mainstream I didn't really think publicly pensioning off The Streets would have the effect it ultimately did. I was doing it more in the hope of encouraging people to notice whatever I went on to do next. So it was a smart thing to do, but maybe not for the reasons people thought. It wasn't about me being a showman. It was simply a pragmatic decision that needed to be taken.

Given how low doing gigs came on my list of priorities when The Streets started (in fact, it wasn't even on the list), the live-led business model we were geared towards by the end certainly represented a big turnaround. But this only reflected a shift in the relative economic significance of live and recorded music which took place throughout the music industry from Napster onwards (and as an enthusiastic patron of Shawn Fanning's pioneering free downloading service myself, it would have been hypocritical of me to complain about its financial consequences for people trying to sell records).

I was lucky that my management were shrewd enough to realize which pie was getting bigger and which one was getting smaller before my record company did, so they could make sure I kept the lion's share of the former while reserving any goodwill gestures for the latter. And as far as The Streets paying our way by being on the road was concerned, not only did that make good semantic sense, it also reflected the deeper understanding of how music works that I'd acquired over the ten years since 'Has It Come To This?'

If you're convinced, as I still am, that the value and power of popular music comes down to the songs, then the performance of those songs in a room (or a field, come to that) is a bit like the transition from making a film to showing a film. It's the first part of that process that takes all the work, but it's the screening in the cinema that you get your money from.

'This isn't one of those Jay-Z or Frank Sinatra type of retirements'

I'd always seen a lot of parallels between what I did with The Streets and the film world. And from acting in videos (which I was surprised to find I was pretty good at) to making our TV show *Beat Stevie* and putting out short films on Twitter, the supplementary activities which have taken up an ever-increasing amount of my time in recent years could be characterized as a pretty useful cinematic apprenticeship. So it's only logical that film should be one field I'm determined to explore now I've shrugged off the expectations associated with The Streets.

I want to find something else that drags me along and that drags other people along with it. I've been excited about that possibility for a long time, but I knew the only way I could do it was to make a fresh start. As The Streets, the things I was best known for were always going to be the things I did at the beginning. There was no way I could be perceived as anything other than a 'legacy artist' — which is the kind way of saying I'm too old to make any difference to the way I'm perceived (other than maybe to make people remember me a bit less fondly by flogging a horse which may not be entirely dead but certainly wouldn't be a good bet to win the Grand National).

When you're the one in front of the camera, you're forced to be a lot more aware of how much age does actually matter. And I think as far as being an MTV or a Radio 1 guy is concerned, thirty is probably where being old starts. Obviously there's the odd exception — by which I don't just mean Susan Boyle — but basically I think you'd be naive to imagine yourself beginning a career in music at that age or older.

It was very apparent to me from my late twenties onwards that

I wasn't someone whose music was going to get played on Radio 1 in the daytime any more. And if you don't find a way of adapting — psychologically, as well as in career terms — to that lack of airplay, you're in danger of getting bitter and twisted about it, like Cliff Richard and Status Quo. If I made a fundamental change at this point — into film, whether via soundtracks or acting or directing — I knew I could find a way of continuing to make new music for the rest of my life, rather than having to scratch a living off past glories.

I've not given up writing songs or producing music or creativity in general. Quite the opposite. What the end of The Streets basically comes down to is that I've retired from rapping. And this isn't one of those Jay-Z or Frank Sinatra type of retirements either. I genuinely never want to rap again.

It's not just me that's got sick of the sound of my own voice. Other people have as well. They've been able to hear it for ten years now, and whether they like it or whether they don't, their opinion is sufficiently set in stone to make it impossible for me to shift it. And if you've got no hope of moving people in one direction, that's the best possible incentive to try and move them in another.

24

You don't really have to stay in touch, because they're going to be there anyway

When I was younger, I always felt like I wanted to be around people more. You can have too much solitude when you're young, and at that point all of your problems in the world seem to stem from the fact that you aren't in enough social situations. But over the years I've come to realize that this was just who I thought I was. You get to a point in your life when you've been around enough people to appreciate that you're actually incredibly solitary by nature.

It would be stretching things a bit to describe this as a recurring theme in my life — I'm not Ernest Hemingway, or Raymond Chandler come to that (though I am a big fan of Raymond's plan to make himself a writer by writing on novel-sized pieces of paper) — but I have always tended to just strike out and move on. When I was sixteen, I went to a college on the other side of Birmingham none of my friends from school had even considered. Three and a half years later, I went to Australia on my own (OK, it was in pursuit of a receptionist, but once I'd caught up with her it only took us a week to break up). Then I came back home and left everyone I knew in the West Midlands behind to move down to London.

I do make friends in each new situation — I'm not anti-social — but I'm always going on somewhere else afterwards. That's probably one of the reasons I've not really sustained many friendships throughout my life. I've never struggled to strike up a rapport with people, there's just something in me that's not very good at staying in touch. And the big thing about family is, you don't really have to stay in touch, because they're going to be there anyway.

Thirty people came to my daughter Amelia's second birthday party, and they were all family. Everyone was related to me or Claire in one way or another. I suppose once you become a bit successful, it's hard to be sure why someone you've just met would want to be your friend, whereas that's not a problem with a cousin who's been taking the piss out of you (and vice versa) since you were a baby. I think there's also a control element in there, which is that I trust my family and don't really want anyone else to know too much about what I'm up to.

I've always liked the idea that I live in my own space, and when I look back at The Streets and the constant opportunities doing that gave me to spend time with people, it's clear that I haven't been out and about nearly as much as the teenage version of me would have imagined I'd have liked to. Around the time of 'Don't Mug Yourself' I think people would have thought of me as someone with quite a hectic social life that was feeding directly into my music, and in a sense that was true, but there were only ever quite a small number of people involved — maybe five.

That number, in terms of how many people I hang about with and see regularly, seems to have held fairly steady ever since, even though the personnel has changed a bit. Even when The Streets were on tour and there were maybe fifteen of us I would get close to the band and a few of the crew, but I wouldn't necessarily know everyone. And that situation would inevitably be shaped by the fact — which I never had a problem with, or really felt awkward about — that everyone else was on a daily wage and I was essentially the boss.

> ⁶ *I actually don't like being around people I don't know* ⁹

When I was growing up, I imagined being around lots of strangers was something I would find really exciting, and I had that experience for a year or so when I was in Australia and really enjoyed it. But having done that enabled me to eventually realize (and it did take several years for this to finally become clear to me) that I actually don't like being around people I don't know.

For a short period in my early to mid-teens, I appreciated the fact that someone was always having a house party where you could go and smoke weed with a lot of other people. By house party, I mean neither a boisterous hip-hop event attended by eighties rappers Kid 'N' Play nor a magical drum-machine-inspired Chicago dance event hosted by Marshall Jefferson and Farley Jackmaster Funk. We're talking about the early nineties here, when the range of formative experiences offered by UK youth culture would probably boil down to going to a small semi-detached house in Stirchley where someone would be playing Utah Saints or EMF very loud on his dad's CD player because his parents had made the mistake of staying away overnight.

These occasions were quite rough and ready, but you generally felt safe going to them. It wasn't exactly gang culture at its starkest, but basically you were over one side of the room with a load of people and there'd be another load of people on the other who you theoretically hated, but it didn't really matter, because everyone was at the party together, and if anything did happen there were twenty of you so it was never a problem. It gave me a lot of confidence to be smoking weed in such large groups. But then there was that incident where the guy who was a boxer had to step in and stop me getting beaten up in the park by people I erroneously believed to be my friends, and at that point I thought, 'Fuck this, I'm going home to make some tunes and I'm not coming back.'

❛ These kinds of generalizations, they don't really read very well ❜

At this point, I'm going to have to venture into an area that some people will probably find a bit controversial. All the time I was getting robbed in the street or on buses as a teenager in Birmingham, it was never white people that did it. It was always kids from Afro-Caribbean backgrounds.

Obviously, the moment you start to make these kinds of generalizations, they don't really read very well. But it's more dangerous not to tell the truth, because it implies there's somehow something to hide, and that leaves people free to think bad things in secret. Which is pretty much what Kelis said on Twitter, when she was talking about the nature of British racism after being racially abused by a guy at an airport.

I never thought black kids in general were more likely to commit crimes than white kids. There was just a cultural difference in terms of the kinds of crimes they tended to opt for once they'd decided to go that way. In my experience, white people who are poor and angry are more inclined to rob houses, whereas street-robbery is more of a black thing. I'm not saying that applies every-where, but it was certainly the way of things in Birmingham in the nineties.

If you wanted to get really dark-side about it, you could say that my whole career is built on mugging black music, and look upon this, from both ways, as some kind of Old Testament eye-for-an-eye scenario. But the fact is that the ethnic division on the larceny side of things was not as stark as it might look on paper. (I hope this statement holds as true for my recording career as it did for my bad experiences on Birmingham's buses, but that's not my call to make.)

I never felt like the kids who were robbing me were doing it because I was white. They were doing it because they could. And the black kids I was friends with were statistically just as likely (if not more so) to get robbed by them as I was.

We all found solace in hip-hop, because that was the one kind of music that seemed to emerge from an understanding of the kind of threatening situations we'd find ourselves in on a daily basis. And the sense of collective security that rap offered — I definitely remember feeling that I got off quite lightly in terms of being hassled after school in my area once I was known as someone who made beats for rappers — was definitely part of its allure.

❛ It wasn't quite like American football ❜

That protective gang mentality I'd experienced briefly earlier in my teens came back for a while when I was seventeen. It seems like a bit of a contradiction, given that being in a gang is expected, almost by definition, to inhibit individual self-expression, but knowing that if you're going out it will probably be in a group of between ten and twenty actually gives you the reassurance you need to be a bit more yourself.

Being on tour with The Streets was the same. I got fairly confident quite quickly about being onstage, because it was a very narrow realm in which I felt like I knew what I was doing, and in that context I could be ebullient and outgoing. It seemed like I was able to interact successfully with thousands of really drunk people, especially in Scotland (which is where I used to enjoy playing live the most), and it would all feel quite controlled. But if you put me in the same venue with the same people and I was in the crowd rather than onstage, I'd probably find that quite intimidating.

Even though it was very much an individual enterprise, for The Streets to function successfully I always depended quite heavily on a supportive group of people around me. It wasn't quite like American football, where the quarterback needs the big blokes around him to run interference, but it wasn't far off.

I'm very passionate about decisions that get made in a work context, and I think I'm particularly drawn to individuals who can control their shit. Presumably I'm attracted to the idea of collaborating with quite well-balanced people because I'm so unbalanced myself. And the fact that a lot of the professional relationships which helped sustain The Streets — with Tim and Ted and Nick Worthington for example — ended up being unusually long-lasting for the music business probably did not reflect any special loyalty on my behalf, but rather my appreciation of how incredibly loyal the people I've worked with have been to me.

‘ *It can end up a bit like* Last Of The Summer Wine ’

Someone once said to me that I seemed to have managed to replicate the supportive social environment my family gave me in a professional context. I'd never looked at it that way, but I suppose there is an element of truth in this suggestion. And the crossover's gone the other way, too.

Now we're talking about making a film, there's a team of us who have a really nice running argument about everything. It's basically me, Ted, and a guy called Sacha who worked on *Beat Stevie* with us. How our system of working together developed was, I'd have an idea and then get side-tracked by having to do some shows or go back to my bunk on the tour-bus for a rest. Then they'd pick it up and run with it and I'd come back to find Sacha wanted me to film a crowd-surfing sequence wearing a suit. I'd tell him I couldn't possibly do that and then he'd say, 'Well, you'll have to.' It was all very harmonious.

It's strange having colleagues who come to your house which is also your place of work. Sometimes it can end up a bit like *Last Of The Summer Wine*. I suppose our Christmas gaming binges are the clearest illustration of that.

When advances in flat-screen technology finally enabled me to play computer games, I didn't feel so much that there was a deficit to be made up, it was more a case of realizing that the reason I hadn't spent all my teenage years playing them wasn't as simple as having epilepsy. There was also something in me that didn't want to waste all my energy on something I wasn't going to get something back from. I do play computer games quite exhaustively over Christmas, though.

You can't get an answer from anyone in the music industry after about 20 December until about 10 January. It's a real shocker. The upside is that in these exceptional circumstances, my Stakhanovite work ethic will allow me a couple of weeks' leave to play computer games. So the studio will be switched off some time around 23 December and the X-Box will go on in its place.

At the time of the first album it was *Age Of Empires* on the PC, and then it was strategy games like *Command & Conquer*. But now it's all about *Call Of Duty* or *Fight Night*. These days there's basically four of us — me, Ted, Magic and Sash — and if we're all in the front room playing *Call Of Duty*, it does feel a bit like a student house.

I have been pondering moving the X-Box into the studio — the advent of a second child (his name is George) can do that to a man. This might sound like the first step on a slippery slope in terms of getting any work done, but even though I buy a lot of games, I rarely touch the console during the year. *LA Noir* is a good example. That's an amazing new game, which I bought on the day it came out and played for an hour or so, but then it was Amelia's bathtime and I've not touched it since.

Reading over these last few paragraphs, I can see that my wife Claire emerges from them as a very tolerant person, which in many ways she is. But she is also used to me being in the studio all the time, so the warlike sounds which accompany a marathon *Call Of Duty* session are not really anything new to her. And when we first met it was on a professional basis, as she was Head of TV Promotions at Warner's, so she knew what she was in for.

If it wasn't for Claire I would long ago have been found wandering down the road near a psychiatric hospital in an NHS dressing gown (if there was such a thing, Ted Mayhem would want one). I said most of this stuff in my groom speech at our wedding. Claire could have been a comedian if she'd been damaged enough in her upbringing to need the attention. I have never seen her not look like a movie star. Her taste in clothes and furniture also seems to have come from some otherworldly school of class I am still taking notes from every day.

The first time I saw her was in Paris, of all places, where I was playing a show at the Triptique. She was probably escorting some showbiz types from a TV channel, trying to convince them that my brand of rhythmical talking was going to work well on *Top Of The Pops* or *T4*. She was wearing a red striped top and I remember thinking she looked amazing but that she would have seen it all before from over excited, sweaty shout singers. Our relationship then developed over time by way of me looking at her a bit funny whenever I saw her, although I didn't really see her that much. She seemed separate from everyone else. Like she was having the real fun, but it wasn't the sort of desperate fun that you just let hang out for everyone to see. It was the classiest fun in town.

We both had to make big changes to be together, and nothing happened between us for a long time. I remember being back-stage with her at *TOTP* and saying, 'let's have a relationship,' but she just smiled and pointed me towards the stage. We weren't an obvious coupling, but three months later we were in Ibiza together, with all my family. We moved in together and never looked back.

I love watching her speak to other people. She manages to make them feel like she is giving them all of her without them feeling like they could have any more. And even though in my songs I prefer descriptions of physical action that imply emotion rather than speaking in abstract concepts like adoration and desire, I'm going to say I love Claire more than anything in the world. I'm looking forward to spending the rest of my life with her. I will get through it by ignoring what she says while paying careful attention to the rest.

Her dad is an engineer, the same as mine (we gave our son their two first names as his middle names, so he's George Ron Alfred Skinner). Another thing Claire and I have in common is that we're both really close to our families.

My dad's death was the first of a series of big shocks to hit my family. His sister Sue died very suddenly of cancer. Almost exactly a year later my niece Chelsea, who was twenty, got run over and killed. Shortly after that both my sisters split up with their husbands. We used to all go out in a large group sometimes; thirty people would come when I played Reading, and we all went to Ibiza together once. It was just an extension of when we were kids, really. We'd all go to Cornwall or the New Forest on holiday and there'd be eight or nine caravans in a ring. It was almost a bit pikey (I'm thinking that's one of those terms you wouldn't use about anyone else, but it's allowed with reference to your own family — kind of like 50 Cent and the N word). Things are much quieter now, but once you've lost a few people it helps you appreciate how much the ones who are left mean to you.

The family members Claire is close to are more of the immediate variety rather than the extended kind like mine. She speaks to her mum and her sister every day on the phone — I think that might be a girl thing — and goes down to see them in Hampshire every couple of weeks or so.

I love it down there.

25

The cliff-hanger at the end of the first one was that Trevor Eve dies, although it turns out he's not really dead

A few months after I turned off The Streets' Twitter feed, I saw the guy from *Silent Witness* (a.k.a. him out of *Shoestring*) on the tube. It was just when that show was coming to an end. There was a two-parter on the Monday and Tuesday, and the cliff-hanger at the end of the first one was that Trevor Eve dies, although it turns out he's not really dead. When you thought he was, though, you (or at least I) experienced a genuine sense of loss, like when John Travolta dies in *Pulp Fiction*: it feels like losing a friend. So for some entirely not rational reason (the obvious parallel with one of the disciples encountering the risen Christ did not hit home until it was pointed out to me a while later), I was well happy to see Trevor, alive and well and hiding behind his *Evening Standard*.

I wouldn't expect people who have listened to the sound of The Streets to feel a similar surge of relief and delight on randomly encountering me on public transport. After all, I've only changed the name I release music under, not put my life on the line in the course of an investigation. But I do have that exciting sense of going back to the drawing board which I assume actors must get when they move on from a role they've played for ages.

Somewhere along the road, I've been fortunate to renew my understanding of what making music for the love of it is. I've always loved the idea of what I was doing, and there was a while back there when I was maybe being led more by the idea than the actual thing. But the first two post-Streets projects I worked on provided me with the perfect opportunity to discreetly dip my toe back into the infinity-pool of artistic self-expression while wearing slightly different swimming costumes.

‘ *I always preferred Ned's Atomic Dustbin* ’

Doing the music for *The Inbetweeners* enabled me to become the kind of producer I'd imagined myself being before The Streets happened — a faceless creator of Ibiza-friendly instrumentals with a cinematic undertow. I was never a teenage film music nerd. I remember once trying to sit through an hour of Vangelis's soundtrack to *Blade Runner* and thinking, with the arrogance of youth, 'What a load of absolute shit.'

This was probably at about the time Pop Will Eat Itself were on heavy rotation at the teenage grebo house parties I was going to (although I always preferred Ned's Atomic Dustbin, if only because I really liked their logo, which was a kind of friendly nuclear waste receptacle with loads of slime around it). And since PWEI's singer and guitarist Clint Mansell has blazed a somewhat unlikely trail for Hollywood film music writers of West Midlands origin, so it would seem churlish of me not to at least attempt to follow in his footsteps.

The other main project I was working on in the immediate aftermath of the end of The Streets was still at the putting-videos-on-YouTube-and-not-really-telling-anybody-about-it phase at the time of writing. It's a band called The D.O.T. with my friend Rob Harvey from The Music who sang on the final Streets album, as well as the last couple of tours. You might have seen us performing together on Alan Carr's *Chatty Man*.

> ❛ *You could say that what they'd done was resolve the Streets/House-boy dichotomy* ❜

We're currently thinking about reactivating The Beats to put out The D.O.T.'s records on. Some people have kindly suggested my label might have been a big influence on UK MCs' subsequent download chart take-over. Maybe we did help pave the way a bit, as a kind of bridge between the Skinnyman and Tinie Tempah eras, but I don't think you can really lump The Beats in with what happened afterwards, because the music changed so much.

The two main factors were, first, a development in confidence, or maybe more accurately in the public's willingness to apprehend it — Professor Green and Example were always confident, it just took people a while to realize. The second and more significant shift was that people got a lot more willing to make what was essentially dance music. At some point, someone had the brilliant idea of getting Tinchy Stryder to rap over a trance tune. It really worked, and then everyone realized it worked, and pretty soon what you were dealing with was a kind of hybrid form of dance music that had been given another name and was now being presented as rap.

Looked at from my own personal point of view, you could say that what they'd done was resolve the Streets/House-boy dichotomy. At this point, Tinie Tempah's 'Pass Out' came along, which was just a really good record. And now this new rap/dance/trance thing is what British rap, at least in commercial terms, is perceived to be.

I've got no problems with that. Even people like N-Dubz, whether you like them or not, they do make something that recognizably does the job of being rap music, just in a very pop way. But I am grateful that I got to make at least my first three albums in a more forbidding and fragmented musical landscape.

‘ Who's to say that Tyler the Creator hasn't felt similar anxieties? ’

If you go to the other end of the hip-hop spectrum and consider someone like Odd Future lynchpin Tyler the Creator, I think what is so compelling about him is his absolute conviction that anything which doesn't sound like him is actually shit. Obviously that belief will fade over time, and in the early stages of someone's career it's hard to tell if there will be anything else there to take its place when that time comes. But for the moment, he's very young, and him and his mates seem to live in their own world which is parallel to but totally unaffected by everyone else's.

Even though this is something which can't actually exist, the illusion of art that only obeys its own rules is a very powerful thing, and even a taste of it is intoxicating — certainly more so than a load of thirty-somethings doing the festival circuit. Whenever you get real excitement of that kind, it generally seems to come from people just under twenty who crop up and they've really got an opinion. You look at them and think, 'Wow, you're not even twenty, and you've really got an opinion.' But then you remember that teenagers actually have way more of an opinion than anyone else does.

When I first started doing interviews as The Streets, I got this sense from all the journalists I spoke to that I was really young (which, compared to them, I probably was) and they were very impressed that I was already so on top of what I was doing. The facts of the situation were that I was never actually going to be any more on top of what I was doing than I was at that moment, I already felt a bit older than I was coming across, and probably 10 per cent of my time was devoted to living the life I spent the other 90 per cent describing (though this was still a higher percentage than a lot of people can manage).

Who's to say that Tyler the Creator hasn't felt similar anxieties? But what mattered more than the facts was the story. And the story was that I was the new thing.

As a young person, new music is always what you're into. You're not into the same things as your parents, you're into change. But because being young is over so quickly, you don't really see it as change, you just think, 'Well, what I like is good and the other stuff is just shit.'

As you get older, though, I think you begin to see how this cycle works. If you talk about a generation as being maybe seven years — in terms of music — you could probably say that The Streets spanned three generations (with the tail-end of UK garage as the first). And by the time you've seen a couple of new ones coming through, you realize that in order to effect these renewals, you have to have people at the front of each wave who are a bit weird.

‘ *I thought artists were wankers* ’

I actually was one of those people, but the thing that gave me my edge was, I didn't know it. In fact, I was determined to think otherwise. I used to hate the word 'artist', and this is probably the thing in my career I've done the biggest U-turn over.

When I did my first album, I loathed the concept of art. I was determined that what I was doing was a craft, and I thought artists were wankers. I still have an ambivalent relationship with the idea of someone calling themselves an artist (in any sense beyond the way they use it on *The X Factor*, where it just means the person singing the song), because it often involves people wasting a lot of time being too self-satisfied. But once a few years had passed after *Original Pirate Material*, I realized that even though what I was doing when I made that album felt very straightforward, and therefore craft-like, at the time, I couldn't do it again, and that's what made it art and not craft.

But without the delusion that what I was engaged in was the latter enterprise rather than the former, I probably wouldn't have been so good at it. My evidence for this proposition is that as soon as I realized that what I was doing actually was art, the whole process got a lot more complicated and difficult.

I would never have said this ten years ago, but if you think about what art actually is, to me it's the newness that is unquantifiable. This is why what really succeeds in art is always what was previously wrong.

That's certainly true of my first album: its greatest strength was that everything about it was wrong. Once you've been party to such a victory-from-the-jaws-of-defeat scenario, there's a temptation to go to the dark side and start deliberately seeking out stuff that's wrong. But that never really works, because the secret of getting it wrong successfully is that — hey Alanis, this one's for you — you were sincerely trying to get it right. Honest failure — that's always the best way forward.

Since I've already scandalized the narrow-minded ghost of my twenty-three-year-old self by giving you my definition of art, I might as well compound the offence with a capsule summation of what creativity means. To me, it must always involve the connecting up of two previously unconnected ideas — at least that's as close as I can get to a working definition.

'You couldn't say any one of them is more Mike Skinner than any of the others'

If you're going to create something that captures people's imaginations, it has to be new; it can't have existed before. There's an outer edge of musical newness which tends to be uncomfortable for a lot of people, then just beneath that there is the comfortably new, which is the big bit. It's like the crust and the mantle, and you want to be in the mantle, really. You can try to formularize that by deciding to take what is really cutting edge and soften it a bit. A lot of A&R men set up camp at that point and do very well out of it, but I'm always more drawn to people whose inclination is to take everything to its logical conclusion.

No one can say I didn't do that with The Streets. There is one aspect of my body of work in that incarnation which I'm proud to think of as reasonably unprecedented. And that's the fact that (and please excuse the lapse into the third person I'm about to be guilty of, but we are in the midst of a crescendo of self-examination here) not only do all of my albums sound like they were made by the same person at every level of the writing and recording process, you couldn't say any one of them is more Mike Skinner than any of the others.

I realize the uniformity of their Mike Skinnerness might be a mixed blessing as far as some listeners are concerned. But there's nowhere in my back catalogue where you'd think, 'Why did he let that be forced upon him?' or 'What was he thinking of working with that producer?' All the fuck-ups are resolutely my own. And I'm happy I managed to keep that going right through to the finish. I can't think of anyone else who's done things in such an auteuristic (some might say autistic) way. Even Eminem doesn't master his own records.

‘ There was definitely a tendency with all the web 2.0 stuff to perceive an egalitarian element that wasn't actually there ’

A lot of huge changes took place in the music industry in the course of The Streets' ten-year life-span. But for all the talk of democratization via the internet, I feel that being on a major record label was more important by 2011 than it had ever been before. Largely because being on the radio had become more important than ever before, and radio more than ever wanted the sure choice.

When it comes to releasing stuff on Twitter, it's obviously much more immediate than the endless painstaking recording process I used to go through: you come up with an idea, write a load of stuff to a deadline, then at six o'clock you just press the button and it's gone. The problem is that if you want something done properly, you by and large still have to do it the old way. Apart from the odd tune done on someone's laptop, the overwhelming majority of releases that actually get into the iTunes chart will have been mixed and mastered in the traditional manner.

Twitter was good for a while, but it's quite time-consuming and stressful, and it kills you in the end because you're constantly reacting all day. Our brains aren't actually designed to conduct conversations with thousands of people at once. That's why people who take to it on a large scale (Stephen Fry is the obvious example) always seem to end up finding out that they just can't handle it any more. It reaches a point where you're hearing so many voices that you might as well be schizophrenic. It probably took about six months after I switched it off for the echoes to die away in my head, but I'd never felt as chilled as I did when that finally happened.

There was definitely a tendency with all the web 2.0 stuff to perceive an egalitarian element that wasn't actually there. A lot of energy went into the whole bringing-down-our-idols-to-a-level-playing-field thing, but that was all bullshit. When I used to ask for outside input, people would say, 'Oh, he's on Twitter and it's all collaborative now', but I never saw it that way. I was just having a laugh.

I would sometimes incorporate the things people sent me, but even if I do that, it's still my song, not your song. Never mind all this hive-mind bollocks. In a thousand years people are still going to be looking to artists and asking them what they say about the world. And your job as an artist is to do good art, it's not to waste your life trying to mollify Americans who can't understand why you won't do more interviews.

Spike Jonze was doing a video for Oasis right at their peak and he pitched this idea to interview a load of people about what they would like to see in the video and then just make that. But actually the stuff people came up with was shit, so they had to ditch it all and do something else instead.

We had a lot of those kinds of experiences. When you put stuff out there and ask people to contribute, the quality of material you get back helps you become aware that this is just a momentary distraction for them, whereas for you it's your whole life. And once the novelty of the collaborative fantasy has worn off, you realize that this is exactly as it should be. If it was their whole life, they'd be working on their own thing, not idling time away responding to yours.

❛ Soft is lighting the whole room and hard is focusing on the one thing ❜

If you want something artistic doing, best pull your finger out and do it yourself. But if someone else's accumulated wisdom can help you, then so much the better. I know some people will look at what I've said about the differences between my first two albums and the music I made after that and think, 'Maybe his later records would've connected with more people if he hadn't filled his head with all those techniques.'

There is obviously an element of truth in that, but the essence of what comes between a person and their original inspiration is that you lose contact with what you like, and that's something that happens anyway, irrespective of how many books on country and western lyric-writing you read. I think I've been way more effective as a consequence of all the knowledge I've acquired. Without it, I'd just have been fumbling around in the dark.

No doubt the same will apply to making films, too. At the time of writing, I'm reading all about cinema lighting. I've got really obsessed with it. The basics are three-point lighting, and beyond that lies the age-old argument about soft versus hard. Soft is lighting the whole room and hard is focusing on the one thing. Three-point lighting is all about fill, hair and key. The key light is the main, brightest one, a fill light evens up the shadows, and a hair light comes from behind and lights up the old barnet (as opposed to New Barnet, which is near where my mum lives).

*

'It's not a question of remembering what Robert McKee says'

I've put a lot of thought into what might be the right closing scene for this book. It's not a question of remembering what Robert McKee says. You've just got to do the stuff that's good and trust that your unconscious is sixteen million times more powerful than your conscious mind. In other words, don't think about it, just do it.

The exterior long-shot is a pub called The Angel in the middle of Highgate Village. The interior close-up is me standing by the bar. And the last line of the screenplay is 'At that point he leaves his three-quarter-full Diet Coke behind him, walks off into the afternoon sun . . . and just does it'.

Index